Amy Mangan

This Side Up

The Road to a Renovated Life

A Memoir

Black Rose Writing | Texas

The final approval for this literary material is granted by the author.

First printing

The author has tried to recreate events, locales and conversations from her memories. In order to maintain anonymity in some instances, the author may have changed the names of individuals and places. The author may have changed some identifying characteristics and details such as physical properties, occupations and places of residence.

ISBN: 978-1-68433-065-2
PUBLISHED BY BLACK ROSE WRITING
www.blackrosewriting.com

Printed in the United States of America
Suggested Retail Price (SRP) $18.95

This Side Up is printed in EB Garamond

To Mike, Griffin and Gillian
Home has always been you.

Contents

Prologue: Show Tunes for an American Nomad

PART ONE: OAK LANE COTTAGE

PART TWO: THE APARTMENT

PART THREE: THE APARTMENT, PART DEUX

PART FOUR: HOUSE OF GRAY

PART FIVE: THE TRI-LEVEL

PART SIX: PARK VIEW

Acknowledgments

This Side Up

Prologue

Show Tunes for an American Nomad

The lake was dry, but I was emptier, sitting on a grassy slope near the shore's edge. I was in my car, an aging one-hundred-and-fifty-four-thousand-mile Chrysler Sebring that hesitated when the ignition was turned on, and which I intended to fix, but had other debts first to pay. It was a Tuesday night in April that was hot, more like the wool blanket of August which typically enveloped this stretch of rural North Central Florida. The lake's remaining water, twelve feet at its deepest, rippled as the sun slowly sank beneath it, as if to wave and invite me in.

All I needed to do was put my car in drive and submerge into the darkness.

I had gone for a ride to clear my head after a long day of fighting battles I was too sapped to face anymore. Clutching the steering wheel, I told myself I'd be okay. Things would get better. Words I'd repeated to my family for the last seven years since we had lost almost everything—jobs that protected us, a home that gave us shelter and fulfillment, health we once took for granted, financial security with hope for our future, and a marriage now shattered like our wedding champagne flutes that had broken when the box they were in fell off the moving truck as we moved to another rental, five houses earlier.

I just needed some space to breathe for a bit. But, a bit turned into hours as I drove north, then east, then west, then north again. It was a familiar route through rolling green pastures dotted with thoroughbred horse farms, moss-covered oak trees and a lake depleted from its former beauty. I had traveled this road as a little girl with my father when we'd go to University of Florida football games. I rode shotgun, a warm bag of boiled peanuts on my lap. Years later, I rode shotgun again, this time with my new boyfriend who opted to drive us an hour north for dinner in Gainesville giving us more time to get to know each other. It worked. We married a year and a half later. On this highway an ambulance had rushed me to deliver my premature son to the university's teaching hospital. The same hospital I'd return to with him twenty years later. The same hospital whose emergency room I had sped to in the middle of the night to be with my daughter.

Why didn't I head south? This path was paved with too many memories piercing my heart with every mile that I drove. My life had been turned upside down since I fell in love with a man who'd take the long way to dinner just to spend more time with me. Who shared my dreams of making a home and a family and setting down roots in the town where we were born.

My hope had disappeared with the other dreams of over two hundred million Americans who were impacted by the country's 2008 economic crash from which pundits said we were recovering. I wasn't so sure. It was the crash that depleted everything I knew to be true and launched a hundred new problems I was ill prepared to fix. A collapse that catapulted me into an often macabre nomadic lifestyle, never being able to stay put in one place no matter how hard I tried. Years of my personal drought had taken their toll.

My eyes stung with tears as the late afternoon evaporated into night. Life was not going as I had hoped. That should be my theme song, I thought driving north. What rhymed with hoped? Coped? Doped? The radio could offer better options. A Broadway song from "The Secret Garden" was playing, not my first choice for a dramatic anthem. The soprano mourned having to leave her loved ones. Not funny, I said aloud, as I turned right onto a country road pulling me toward a stranger's house by Orange Lake.

By the time I reached the lake, it was just light enough for me to see that this once-rich basin of life had been affected by the harsh elements of an extended dry spell. I remembered reading about it in the local newspaper in interviews with business owners around the lake who had suffered losses during the parched years.

"The last seven years have been a disaster," said a fish camp owner, noting most of the camps were now out of business. "I'm not a fish camp anymore. I'm just a rental community."

Often I thought of how so many Americans had become part of a rental nation, leasing homes, lives and short-term stability until the next crisis hit. Home became a euphemism for the life I had dreamed of, not the one I lived. And I knew all about home. I wrote about it extensively in a past life as a home and garden editor. Once, I was a writer. And a wife. And a mother who'd make "Just Because" homemade cupcakes to celebrate an ordinary day with two beautiful children. Now I was incapable of keeping them healthy and whole.

Looking in the rearview mirror, I didn't recognize the woman who used to be all those things. The view behind me was blocked, literally, with large moving boxes stacked up to the top of the car. I'd picked them up from a packing store in case our current landlord decided he would not be able to let us rent for another year. We'd already negotiated an extra year when we'd extended our lease last summer. I couldn't imagine packing again. I was drained, weary from fighting to stay afloat while trying to plug the oceanic hole of yet another challenge in front of me.

But the lake was in front of me, too.

"How could I know I would have to leave," sang the musical's desperate heroine on the radio. How could she? How could I? Turning off my cell phone, I could only think of the collective misfortunes of my life. I questioned if I had made them better or worse. And I thought of my family. My husband. My sweet, tender and resilient son and daughter. They had been through so much. So much unsolicited pain. Numbed by the anesthesia of grief for the life I could never seem to adequately manage, I chose the only path right in front of me.

I put the car in drive.

PART ONE: OAK LANE COTTAGE

Chapter 1

The Side Entrance: Ode to Spode

Glancing out the side entrance to our home, I yelled to my family—and anyone else within a five-mile radius—as the big delivery truck pulled into our driveway.

"They're here!" I shouted. "The packages have come!"

Christmas was in the air that day even though Thanksgiving was still a week away. After signing the delivery slip, I placed the two large boxes on the leather ottoman in the family room. Just looking at the packages gave me goose bumps. I was like Darrin McGavin in *The Christmas Story* movie when the lamp he'd ordered, shaped like a woman's leg, arrived in a large box on his doorstep. Tearing open the first box, I squealed at the sight in front of me.

"Oh, how beautiful," I whispered reverently as I pulled several crème-colored ceramic dishes from the plastic bubble-wrap. They were painted in a rich brown and beige design. I wasn't sure that fine china and a back porch normally went hand-in-hand from a decor perspective, but it didn't matter. Soon, everything would come together. I just knew it.

My family and I had recently moved into the two-story brick cottage at the end of an oak-lined road in Florida. Oak Lane Cottage, our family's third home, had a neglected screened-in porch with brick paver flooring and was the only one we'd ever formally named, as if our bequeathing a title to a structure guaranteed certainty. But we were sure about this house. This was *the one.* We had been like Goldilocks in our quest for the perfect home.

Our first place with no name had been Mike's late great Aunt Cristina's ranch-style house that had been his thirty-six-year-old bachelor pad, until his new twenty-six-year-old bride moved in. It was too small. And very late great aunt in décor with yellow shag carpet, tiny musty-smelling rooms, and 1970s-era green linoleum flooring in the kitchen, the laundry room and the family room, where it curled up at the edge of the wall exposing the concrete slab. I believe Aunt Cristina would've floored the garage with linoleum if she could have.

With the addition of Griffin and Gillian, we moved into Mike's late mother's home in a different neighborhood in a good school district. This home was bigger, but had a challenging floor plan. The master bath, which was the size of a small coat closet, opened directly into the family room with an unreliable sliding pocket door as the divider. Things got awkward when guests were over and someone used the bathroom. I would talk loudly or turn up the TV volume in the family room to drown out the sound of the toilet flushing or some flatulent noise on the other side of the sliding door. We renovated and rejuvenated as best we could, but it always felt like the home of another Mangan relative.

A half a mile away in the same neighborhood we discovered a Cape Cod-style cottage for sale at the end of a road nestled by large grand oak trees with branches that intertwined like an old lady's fingers and let the sun filter in through her canopied hands. The house had lots of potential. A large back yard with room for the kids to play. A kitchen that had good bones and was ripe for a Mangan re-do. And three fireplaces! After closing at the title company, Mike and I drove straight to the house among the oaks. Holding hands, we walked in the front door where Mike proclaimed this was the house we would grow old in.

It was just right.

Well, almost right. I made a home renovation notebook of the projects I wanted to take on. Kitchen renovation. Master bath expansion. New paint for the bedrooms. Front yard landscaping. Window treatments. New paint for the dining room. Downstairs bedroom-to-library conversion. New paint for the family room. Hell, new paint for *every* room. I included a section in my notebook for the back porch update that would eventually, I knew, be the piece de resistance of my decorating dreams.

My life became full-throttle nesting. I set out to transform this house and collected the things you collect when you say you are making a place of your own—new art for the paneled walls, lamps for the living room, and tchotchkes for tables and shelves because a house isn't a home without a brass monkey holding a candle. But our porch budget was limited, so the porch consisted of two lawn chairs.

Longing for a place to retreat, I entered a home decorating contest sponsored by *Better Homes & Gardens Creative Home,* one of the many "shelter" magazines I read. Lo and behold, I won a complete porch makeover by the magazine's very own editor, and their team flew in from Iowa and spent four days painting, building, wiring, accessorizing and furnishing my porch. Pure nesting bliss. The results featured a hand-painted dining table, two luxurious outdoor-friendly chaises with matching chenille blankets and needlepoint pillows, an antique white sideboard that I helped build, and not one but *two* crystal chandeliers hanging over my dining table. The wrought-iron dining chairs had custom-made tufted seating. I even had white gauze curtains hanging from each end of the porch.

Curtains. *On my porch.*

No beautifully appointed porch is complete without accessories and I had those in spades, or rather, Spode. The magazine editor had chosen a brown-and-beige theme for the porch, and she shipped in boxes of Spode china —plates, tea cups, pitchers—in a matching palette and one silver-plated metal dessert server to hold three Spode dessert plates.

The plates depicted nineteenth century scenes commissioned by a man named Spode Copeland who was rather fond of fine china and unique, long-ago landscapes. One plate had a sketch of two full-figured women lounging on an ornate Greek columned porch—kind of like my sister and I, minus the lounging and ornate part. Another plate showed two soldiers fighting to hold onto what appeared to be a pig that was clearly not cooperating with its captors.

I had never heard of brown transferware—a most unusual description of china—and yet I wondered where it had been all my life. Mike would come home that night to enjoy seeing his usually loquacious wife dumbstruck. By a plate.

An hour after Spode had come into my life by way of Fed Ex, I remained parked on my couch carefully unpacking the china. Gillian and Griffin joined me around the ottoman and we yelped every time we pulled out another piece from the boxes.

"Look at this, mama!" Gillian said as she held a miniature Spode pitcher.

"Here's another one!" Griffin said while unwrapping a plate.

"We should play Christmas music," I joked as I dug into a box to pull out another treasure. The pile of bubble-wrap grew so high on our family room floor that we had to do a search and rescue mission to find our dog, Honey, who had been buried beneath it.

"Hey! Honey matches the china!" Griffin said laughing at our brown-and-white Chi-Poo who had begun jumping on the bubble-wrap as it pop-pop-

popped like a firecracker. Clicking on my iPod, I found our Mangan Christmas playlist.

"Why not?" I asked aloud and began dancing around the ottoman of porcelain treasures while Bing Crosby crooned about glistening tree tops and sleigh bells in the snow.

This space was the heart of our house, mainly because visitors came through the side entrance more often than the front door. We'd tell friends to come to the "second front door" when visiting. To match the brick paver floor, the room boasted a matching brick fireplace and bookshelves next to it where I kept every board game imaginable. My mom had given me a dark-stained side table that fit perfectly in between the couches and I placed a large lamp on it for ample light.

Our kitchen and back porch were connected to this space so the second front door was a direct shot to constant activity and foot traffic. And the best place for celebrations. Sometimes the party began *outside* the side entrance where a wooden bench had been placed next to the second front door and served as the spot to drop off packages and baseball and volleyball team jerseys.

After the makeover was complete and magazine photos had been taken, I invited friends, neighbors and family over to sip some wine and see our newly decorated porch. The magazine's makeover crew agreed to stay for the party, joking they had never been to a "sip and see," which led me to wonder if they had ever been to the South before.

In time, the silver-plated dessert server would not stay on the porch. I moved it inside where it became a running joke among friends for the many uses I had created for it. Some days the server held pastel-sprinkled mini cupcakes for birthdays. Other days it made a most convenient spot for serving bite-size appetizers after it had been given an instant promotion from the kitchen counter to the kitchen island, the epicenter of our world. Later I moved the server to my home office, a former den I had created as a place of my own to write and read, and write a little more if I was lucky. The server became my office supply accessory and held pens and pencils on one plate, paper clips on another, and a stapler on the last.

The server—with its nineteenth century scenes of lounging women and escaping pigs— had a French inscription beneath the capture-the-pig painting, "Tiens Fermé," which, translated, means "Hold On." I remember noticing those words for the first time when it was Christmas in November in our side entrance room.

"What does this mean?" Gilly asked pointing to the plate's inscription.

"I have no idea," I said shaking my head.

Soon, however, those words would come to bear significant meaning, when the only thing I could do was hold on tight.

Chapter 2

The Back Porch: Like No Tomorrow

By the night of my porch "sip and see" in the fall of 2003, I had checked off most of Oak Lane's fixer upper projects. I liked checking things off my list. "Order breeds serenity" was my favorite mantra.

"What breeds serenity, kids?" I'd ask Griffin and Gilly when we were cleaning up their rooms.

"Order!" They would yell, laughing and visibly ribbing their orderly mom, as they stopped to play with a toy before putting it away.

At thirty-eight years old, a sense of order was reigning supreme in my life. I was a history professor at the local community college and that afforded me the flexibility to teach when the children were in elementary school and be home when they were. My work schedule also gave me time to pursue freelance writing with a local magazine.

Mike had dreams, too. Just before we moved into Oak Lane, he had left the family business he'd been in for over twenty years, running a local insurance agency, to work for a metal roofing company that promised greater financial and professional security. The housing market was booming and houses needed roofs.

And, an hour before guests had arrived to our porch party, the magazine editor who had just finished styling my new porch buffet with Spode china, asked me if I'd like to write the magazine story of my porch reno. This would be my first article in a national publication. Let the party begin!

Mom and Dad arrived first, typically early. Walking into our foyer, Dad handed me a CD of music he'd made to commemorate the evening with some of our favorite singers—Sinatra, Washington and Bennett—the big band trinity of cool and classic. Dad's pressed blue cotton shirt hung on his thin frame. Decades of heart disease had robbed him of good health and stamina, but nothing was going to stop my eighty-one-year-old father from celebrating his baby girl's party. I took my gift to the CD player on the sideboard and smiled as the opening strains of "I've Got the World on a String" played.

Dad slowly walked through the kitchen to the back porch, surveying the room before sitting on one of the two upholstered sage green chaises. I wanted him to love it as much as I did. Though he was retired now, he could lay claim to having erected many of our hometown's residential and commercial structures. And I was Sherman Yeary's daughter.

Mom was forty when she gave birth to her fourth child, a feat she labeled a "blessing and miracle." I had to remind my three older sisters of that each time they would pick on their "blessing and miracle" and give me underwear wedgies before heading into church on Sundays. My sisters were Phase One of the Yeary family plan, spanning a seventeen-year gap between Donna, the oldest, to me, the youngest. Julie and Cindy served as the middle siblings rounding out the Yeary girls of Ocala, Florida. When Cindy moved out of our home at age nineteen, I was eight years old, ripe for mom's and dad's undivided attention. For Dad this meant a chance to mold me into a budding builder, and I was a willing protégé.

Tagging along with Dad at his work site was as good and pure a life as I could imagine. I'd watch in rapt attention as he'd prepare to drive a nail into a two-by-four. He was the Houdini of hammering, clenching his teeth around the smallest nail while managing to hold a hammer, pencil and level without dropping—or swallowing—anything.

Dad made sure I had my own toolbox. The bright red metal container held dividers full of Dad's hand-me-down screws and nails with a clunky measuring tape and a rusty wooden hammer. As a child, I lugged that thing around Dad's construction sites, ready to help him in case his crew of twenty men couldn't find any of their tools. Dad indulged his young apprentice by asking me to measure a window or borrowing my one and only Phillips-head screwdriver. Tightening a bolt, he'd hum the Sinatra tune "You Make Me Feel So Young."

One of the best gifts Dad gave me came from scraps. After cleaning up a finished project, he used a pile of discarded doors to build my very own playhouse. The side panels were composed of hollow-board hallway doors running horizontally, knobs intact. The roof was a mismatch of asphalt shingles. And Dad had managed to salvage a bathroom sink for my faux kitchen inside. He placed a glass-paneled walnut door as the entryway. It looked like Dorothy's house, post-tornado, from *The Wizard of Oz*, but I loved that place like no tomorrow.

While most fifteen-year-old girls were reading *Seventeen* magazine and listening to K.C. and the Sunshine Band, I was poring through house plans. Dad gave me one of his spare drawing boards, which I would prop on my bed and make sketches of my dream room. One drawing included an elaborate floor-to-ceiling bookcase dividing the bed from the door, a design that looked like I.M. Pei had married Alice in Wonderland. Always encouraging, Dad gently pointed out I had blocked the door's entryway with the bookshelves. Eventually, it became apparent that measurement skills were not my strong suit. I would not become an architect or a builder, but I would always be one fine assistant to Dad, local builder, mentor and house-of-doors designer.

My toolbox got good use throughout the years. I took it to college to hang framed posters on my dorm walls and to assemble a cheap TV stand in my first apartment.

When I was lucky, Dad would bring his tools and help me out. We were a dynamic remodeling duo. One weekend when Mike was out of town for a golf tournament, Dad came over to our newlywed home. I showed him a nascent wall dividing the dining room and the living room and blocking my much-desired view of the backyard. Dad knocked his fist up and down the wall.

"Shoot, this isn't load bearing. We can take it down," Dad said.

And so we did. That very same day.

We hadn't exactly thought through what would happen after we knocked out the wall with our matching sledgehammers. I now had a wide open gap of the concrete floor along the shag carpet, where the wall had once stood. And we would need to plaster the ceiling and the remaining rough edges on the side. But it was another completed father-daughter project and we were happy and already scheming our next reno. Dad and I later added a faux fireplace in that same house, and we built a bench that framed the swimming pool deck at the next one. We installed new lighting over the dining room table there, too. We probably violated every electrical code in the book, but it sure looked good.

By the time I moved into Oak Lane, however, Dad was no longer the vibrant, big band-singing builder whose hugs smelled of sweat and sawdust. His heart was giving out. Just getting dressed each day was a big deal. He had relinquished his builder's tools to his backyard shed several years earlier.

When the magazine crew arrived at our home three days before the big porch reveal, I went to the garage and dusted off my worn and faded metal toolbox that

Dad had given me so many years earlier. With the rusty wooden hammer, I returned to the screened-in porch ready for an assignment.

The editor handed me the patina iron wall hanging. Clenching a nail in my teeth while measuring the spot to hang it, I thought of Dad. And my all-door playhouse. And my borrowed days back on my construction sites. For a moment, I wondered if I now had borrowed days in my home among the oaks. I quickly dismissed the thought.

My wall hanging was level. Dad, my keen supervisor and mentor, would approve, even as he was dying in front of me sitting on my chaise that night of the party.

Mom, the consummate caregiver, brought Dad a plate of baked brie and table water crackers that he nibbled on as others arrived. The unseasonably cool late November afternoon and the good company seemed to rally Dad. He was one of the last guests to leave, yet I suspected it was the notion of the well-done design plan that had best lifted his spirit.

Our porch had been overflowing with people and Pinot Grigio. The fragrant sweet smell of fresh cut roses on my hand-painted dining table perfumed the crisp fall air. The magazine editor and her handy team of helpers mingled as we clinked our wine glasses with a toast to their beautiful handiwork. I had never seen anything so lovely.

They had painted the porch's metal ceiling a subtle light green to complement the chaise lounges. Two crystal chandeliers were hung from my subtle green ceiling that reflected a soft light as the sun set beneath the oak trees in our backyard. Large sisal rugs hugged the brick floor. A stately boxwood topiary in an ebony porcelain urn stood next to the concrete wall between the porch and the family room. Customized brown toile fabric draped a newly built sideboard with elegant china, roses and my CD stereo playing Dad's big band bests on top.

And those curtains. What was once an eyesore of a worn-out screen had become a focal point. I had helped hang weather-resistant muslin drapes, which matched the sideboard, on the screened walls to hide an unsightly air conditioner. Nearby, two patina iron works hung on the wall behind my luxurious chaises, now draped in chenille blankets and needlepoint pillows. The color theme was sage green, brown and pink.

Who had a color theme on their friggin' porch? I did.

It was almost too much. I was giddy from it all and from probably a tad too much Pinot. Then there was the Spode china. Oh. My. Gawd. Perfect. Simply perfect. That magical night, I felt like I could touch the sky but still be grounded by a warm contentment of gratitude and love.

Everyone oohed and aahed over the porch on that cool November evening. I told all my friends how easy it actually was to hang curtains on a porch and how to build a buffet from scratch. Dad smiled at his youngest daughter's interest in home remodeling and commented, tongue-in-cheek, how useful "that three-leveled plate stand is gonna be" in my life. Mock away, I said. Nothing could dampen my spirits. I now had Spode in my life. And chandeliers. And chaises to lounge on while gazing at my gauze curtains.

Tall hurricane glasses held vanilla-scented candles placed on the table and sideboard. Everything glowed, me included. My neighbors, who lived across the street, would later build a similar sideboard that they placed in their kitchen. Friends decided crystal chandeliers were a good idea on their porch. Even two of my sisters, who were not design inclined, agreed candles really could finish a room and bought a few for their own homes. My cottage had inspired a local home décor cottage industry.

It was one of the most blissful nights of my life. I had everyone and everything I needed. Mike and I weren't financially as secure as we had hoped, but we had potential, a new job for Mike and a new writing assignment for me, one that would give me street cred to secure other national magazine stories. I actually would be paid to write about home—my home—the thing, the concept, the dream I loved as deeply as anything next to my family.

After everyone left, Mike, Griffin, Gilly and Honey and I ended up back on the back porch. It was a our own post-event high as Mike and I recounted the events of the evening.

"Wasn't Patty funny as she measured our sideboard?" Mike asked.

"I think everyone had a good time," I said, taking it all in. "Can you believe this is our porch?"

Mike grinned and shook his head. He was silent, as if not to utter the very thing I was thinking. This was too good to be true. I once had a pillow on my bed with the inscription "Too much of a good thing is wonderful." But, were we realistic?

Grif and Gilly fell asleep on the chaises, blankets pulled up to their chests. Honey was snoozing on the sisal rug. I had bought a bottle of really good champagne at the grocery store earlier that day when I had gone out to get pink roses for my newly acquired Spode brown transferware. While Mike cleaned the dishes, I popped the cork to open the chilled champagne and poured the bubbly wine into glass flutes. Dad's CD was on its umpteenth replay rotation, but I didn't care. I had so much to celebrate.

"To us," I toasted.

"To us," Mike tipped his glass.

"May we always love this place like no tomorrow."

The very act of uttering this thought, this fervent hope, seemed risky. If I said aloud a dream, would it go away?

The champagne started to sour in my stomach. I worried, a skill I had acquired early in my marriage and had honed like an athlete. Some people did Cross Fit. I fretted. We'd already been tested in our marriage. Marrying a confirmed bachelor required adjustments for us both. Then Griffin was born two months prematurely with a six-week hospital stay, almost succumbing to viral meningitis. He was now a strapping eight-year-old boy sleeping next to his six-year-old little sister on a porch with chandeliers and curtains. Things were better. More certain.

What a world, what a life we now had.

I picked up the portable stereo and moved it from the porch back to the library, a former bedroom I had converted into my personal work space. Calling it a library seemed indulgent, but so did naming a house. As much as I loved my newly decorated back porch, the library was my favorite room. I felt safe there. I had lined the walls with shelves for my books and had still run out of space, leaving stacks of books on the floor. It was the one place I could escape and get lost in a novel until I nodded off in my chair.

My desk in the library, my grandmother's dining table, is where I would soon begin my full-time writing career. It would also be the room where I would learn that the world and life I had so carefully constructed, the one that included the luxurious back porch, was coming to an end.

Chapter 3

The Library: Infinite Riches

I converted the downstairs guest bedroom into my library by painting the walls and store-bought bookshelves a neutral light gray color—Benjamin Moore's "Revere Pewter"—so my books would be the room's focal point. No dark paneled wood for me, I wanted light and bright. It was no Library of Congress, but my books, many I'd owned since graduate school, finally had a home.

My desk was centered in the room, the "floating technique" I'd read about in a design magazine. It was surrounded by the works of my favorite writers, Pat Conroy, Winston Churchill, Billy Collins, Anna Quindlen and Eudora Welty. I moved a recliner from the family room into the library next to my floating desk and sometimes I would just sit there, taking it all in, my Paul Revere home office/library. I actually had a room of my own, thank you, Virginia Woolf and Benjamin Moore.

Evenings in the library were best. After the children fell asleep in their upstairs bedrooms, I'd quietly walk down the wood staircase to my light and bright library, pull a book off the shelf, curl up in my recliner, sip a cup of Chamomile tea and read. The more I read, the more I wanted to write and I finally had the perfect space to do it. Since the porch makeover, writing had poured out of me like a faucet that wouldn't turn off. I wrote essays, editorials, columns for magazines and newspapers. A friend generously created a website for my work. I wrote the first draft of my novel, too.

My porch story, which was published in the *Better Homes and Gardens* specialty magazine, had served as a springboard to writing for *Southern Living* and *Southern Accents* magazines. The latter gave me a regular feature called "A Sense of Place," editing famous writers who contributed essays about where they lived.

Somebody pinch me.

This inspired me to leave my college teaching job to accept a full-time associate editorial role at a city magazine. Knowing my fondness for decorating, my editor gave me the chance to develop special sections featuring home makeovers and projects. All because, five years earlier, I took a chance and entered a home renovation contest while sitting at my desk island enveloped by Pat, Winston, Billy, Anna and Eudora. The library was my good luck charm.

My luck got better in early 2008. I had almost finished editing a home and garden book for the magazine, a first of its kind for the publisher and me. This project, *The Style Book, Volume One*, was my baby. My colleagues and friends said it had "Amy written all over it." My library overflowed with baskets of shelter publications, all the magazines about home design, renovation and landscaping. I liked saying I was in the biz, specifically the shelter publishing biz, which afforded me the fantasy of swapping editorial ideas and photos shoot concepts with the likes of Martha Stewart and Candice Olsen.

The Style Book was all about an "innate sense of style," a description I wrote in my editorial welcome letter with a photo of me sitting very authorly in a Chippendale leather chair while holding a book. Before the photo shoot, I splurged on a new chocolate brown velvet jacket and pressed jeans and then went to the hair salon. Florida humidity was never kind to my wiry middle-aged hair and this photo would call for a professional.

My picture was taken at a photography studio, home of the leather chair. The photographer had suggested I bring a book to capture an informal look of me reading, as if I typically read at home wearing a crushed velvet jacket and pressed jeans with rockin' tamed bangs. I brought Will Durant's *The Story of Civilization; Our Oriental Heritage, Volume One*, the first of eleven in his famous series covering Western history from the beginning of civilization to the nineteenth century. The photographer looked at me.

"Seriously?" He asked, holding the book. "A little light reading, huh?"
I took the book and sat in my chair in front of the photo drop cloth. Slowly I ran my fingers across the maroon-colored linen book cover with the gold metallic title. For a moment, I was twenty-four again.

Inside the front cover was my signature—Amy Yeary—written in blue ink in large curly cursive with an inventive interpretation of the letter "A" that looked like a stick-figure step-ladder with a loose rope around its middle. That letter had nothing on the "Y's," however, with the bottom loops so large you could draw a face in them. I'd practiced my signature for most the late 1980s as if a young community college history professor, fresh out of graduate school, would have reason to autograph frequently.

The Durant series was a coveted purchase after graduation, inspired from university courses where reading Durant was the intellectual litmus test. I ordered them with my first teaching paycheck. Each volume averaged nine hundred pages and I made it a goal to read every volume by the time I was forty because that was, like, eons away.

Until it wasn't eons away anymore.

I got to Ancient Greece and stopped reading. I thought Durant went a little overboard on the history of the Sumerian potter's wheel, but maybe I was being picky.

I loved Durant's personal story as much as I loved his work. In his 1935 preface, he adapted a rather optimistic tone for someone who was about to dedicate a serious chunk of his life to this project. He said he hoped his work would help future readers understand and enjoy "the infinite riches of their inheritance."

Sitting beneath the hot photo studio lights, I thought of my infinite riches.

Mike and I had been married for eighteen years, two rare Ocala natives who had found each other after returning home from out-of-town colleges and jobs.

Griffin and Gillian were thirteen and eleven, exploring the world of adolescence in their own ways. Griffin was in eighth grade, preparing for high school because I blinked and he had grown into an introspective teenager who had discovered the magic a guitar makes when it's properly strummed. And Gilly found her own kind of magic on a volleyball court, turning a gym sport into a year-round club passion.

We had lived in Oak Lane for five years and it was everything we'd hoped it to be. More, really. It became an extension of our family, and we talked about Oak Lane as if it were a sibling or a really cool aunt. It was our safe base, our source of joy in every nook and space. I hung a brass plaque with "Oak Lane Cottage' next to the front door. It was official—we were home.

And I was doing okay as a healthy forty-four year old in decent shape with modestly broad hips managed by the occasional use of Spanx. And I was posing in a fancy chair for a photo shoot. My inaugural publication was one I had help to create, write and edit, including interviews with some of the best in the design industry, including Candice Olsen.

Infinite riches!

Ocala had long been a unique and wealthy equestrian enclave in Florida, home to multimillion dollar estates on rolling pastureland. This was not typical palm trees-and-tourists Florida. This was home to thoroughbred horses where Triple Crown winners were trained and industry thrived with the area's proximity to the interstate. Ocala and Marion County were situated just far north enough in the state, away from Miami and Orlando, and just removed enough from the coastal beaches, that Southern culture was alive and well—a perfect environment for graceful and elegant homes. I envisioned the book as an editorial home tour offering a glimpse into some of Ocala's most beautiful residences as if the reader were walking through each room.

From start to finish, the book took about six months to develop and publish. I'm Southern so I'm nosy. This gig was the perfect job for a nosy Southern editor who also happened to be a huge fan of home and garden stories. Someone, probably one of those HGTV designers whom I envied, once said our home is our masterpiece. I wanted to show readers how they, too, could turn their homes into masterpieces, with big and small solutions. In a way the book was my personal masterpiece, too, layering my passions, friendships and dreams into a grander portrait—well, into a soft-bound one hundred and sixty-page publication with limited distribution. But, yet!

It was something. And it was *my* something.

The Style Book, Volume One was celebrated with an early summer cocktail book signing at the magazine's office. The tiny space near Ocala's historic downtown district was filled with guests lined up to get their copy of the glossy book. Our writers autographed their respective authored chapters while the featured homeowners quickly flipped through the pages to find their own stories. The wine and praise flowed. The editorial team surprised me with a framed shadowbox of the book. Everyone applauded as I accepted my gift, my version of an Oscar of Best Performance for A Local Home and Garden Editor of a Book with Limited Distribution.

It was a perfect evening, my masterpiece.

I was fired by the publisher the next week.

"Money is tight," she said.

It was?

"We're cutting back and it's not about you," she insisted. "We love your work."

Yes, I know. I had a framed shadowbox with my name on it. She said other things, but the ringing in my ears insulated me from hearing the high praise I was receiving while being promptly dismissed.

There would be no Volume Two. Durant had spent more time writing about Sumerian ceramic making than I had lasted in the shelter publishing biz.

I took solace that Mike now had a good job at Merrill Lynch. His roofing career was short-lived, but he quickly found a financial advisor position with one of the most successful investment management corporations in the country. For almost three years, Mike had worked hard to build his client portfolio and had passed the rigorous securities broker license examination on his first try. He adapted easily into the complex world of stocks, bonds and hedge funds and other things I didn't completely understand, but I knew this was a field that had yielded great financial rewards for many of our friends, some of whom were now Mike's work colleagues.

He was late in the game to try this career at the age of fifty-two, but he worked hard, showed up at the office before most and left late. His clients trusted him with protecting their valuable assets. Mike knew this and took his job seriously. It was high stakes in Mike's new role, both for him and his clients, an industry based on risk and reward.

However, as if having a newly-unemployed wife wasn't stress enough, Mike was feeling a new pressure from his job. Merrill Lynch had recently replaced its previous CEO, Stan O'Neal, with a high energy executive, John Thain, formerly of the New York Stock Exchange. And with high energy came high expectations that resonated throughout the company, especially to financial advisors like Mike. Thain had arrived in late 2007 to turn things around for Merrill after a disappointing performance in the third quarter due to the development of what appeared to be trouble on the horizon: sub-prime mortgages.

Mike, the calm optimist, tried to reassure me. Thain's arrival to Merrill was a positive step in the right direction, he said. He believed Thain was an effective leader for what was becoming a perilous time in the financial industry. Thain would right the ship in rough waters, he'd tell me. In that year Mike had spoken of John Thain so often that our children thought he was a co-worker who sat in the cubicle across the hall from their Dad.

One late afternoon in September, three months after I had lost my job, I was sitting in my recliner in the library chatting on the phone with my friend Sara while the children were doing their homework at the kitchen island. A thunderstorm was about to fall open over the house, with thunder and lightning so loud, Sara and I decided we should end our call.

"Wait, Amy, did you hear the news about Merrill Lynch this afternoon?" she asked.

"No, what happened?" I asked, almost afraid to hear.

"They are merging with Bank of America. Sounds like they have to," she said.

Sara was my informed friend, staying up on current events. She also knew her friend on the other end of the phone was struggling post-firing to find her footing. I had been unemployed since July searching for another job.

I hung up the phone and ran upstairs to turn on the television in our master bedroom. I didn't want to alarm the kids. Thain was on all the networks saying the merger was a good thing. It would help both companies quell the financial storm. I called Mike. He was unaware of the merger. His good friend John Thain had failed to inform most of Merrill's employees.

"Will you be okay?" I asked Mike as my heart pounded in my chest like a hammer on a nail. I closed the bedroom door in case one of the children came upstairs.

"I think so," Mike said, "This will be a good acquisition."

"What if it isn't?" I asked. "What will happen to you?"

"Amy, we can't live our lives in fear," Mike said.

Which is exactly how I lived mine for the next three months, consuming myself with adrenaline-fueled fear. A friend once said to me that fear is a gift. I made it an ever-present big honking package wrapped in a bow of obsessive dread. Even good news was blighted by my uneasiness.

I found a community relations job at the public library, grateful to have found something, but anxious about the change my work schedule would have on Griffin and Gilly. They were both in middle school, not the ideal time to become latch-key kids, but my new job did not afford me the flexibility I once had as a magazine editor. And Mike couldn't help out. He was working longer hours at the office hoping to prove he was worth keeping, post-merger.

Throughout this time, Mike kept telling me how John Thain would fix Merrill Lynch though the news media begged to differ and hinted that Thain might be a bigger part of Merrill's problems than originally thought. Mike kept his faith in the Merrill CEO right up until the week before Christmas when he lost his job, five months after I had lost mine.

The sub-prime mortgage field had become a full-blown crisis. Merrill, hemorrhaging from bad defaults, mortgages and plummeting stock prices, fired employees in Mike's position who had been with the company on average less than three years.

Mike had been with Merrill for two years and eleven months.

We thought we had been bold and brave in our choices to start new careers that promised good fortune in intangible and tangible ways. Now we were unemployed, unsure about our future and our children, whose riches suddenly seemed finite, limited, with an uncertain, precarious inheritance.

Earlier that December, my sister had mailed me some of my old magazine clippings. She was our family collector and kept things like her sister's writings. She still used the postal system to mail them to me even though we lived in the same town. One of the clips was a column called "The Media File" that I had written for the magazine back in 2006, two years before *The Style Book* came out. I'd forgotten about that column in which I'd offered reading suggestions. The article featured a picture of me smiling directly into the camera while standing and holding books.

Again with the books.

There they were, four big-ass maroon-linen books with a gold metallic title on the sides. My shoulders were slumped forward from the weight of holding them, like I was a volunteer at the local library book sale schlepping old books to a buyer's car. They were four volumes of Durant's series—I couldn't make out which titles—but it looked like some of his more beefy ones, like his one thousand-paged *Rousseau and Revolution, Volume Ten.* Why did I always bring those damn things to photo shoots? I had hundreds of other books on my shelves.

Maybe because Durant had been with me all along. Graduate school. First paycheck. Single girl apartment. Boyfriends. Teaching. Marriage. Children. First home as a married couple, then second, now, Oak Lane. Those books were often the only permanent thing about me.

I lugged world history wherever I went. Durant concluded his life's work with the French Revolution admitting he may have overcommitted to documenting the past. By the time he got to the big one in France, he had run out of time to write any further. Durant had made a valiant effort. He wanted to get it right. It goaded him when other historians only looked at a piece of history and not the whole picture. He was shooting for the whole enchilada as a way of explaining things.

The Style Book was no sweeping assessment of why we lived the way we did, though I tried to catch a glimpse of it. In my welcome letter—the one with the photo of Woman with Book Sitting in Leather Chair—I said I hoped the book would celebrate all that was special about Ocala's homes and the people who lived in them. I wanted to look inside, room by room, and not just give a passing glance.

I wanted to capture the whole enchilada. With the book, my job, my family, my dreams. Yet by Christmas of 2008, everything was wrong. My editorial job was gone and Mike's was too. While seven hundred select Merrill employees were awarded end-of-the year bonuses that totaled over three billion dollars in a year the company had lost twenty seven billion dollars, Mike was not one of them. He was unemployed with a two-week paycheck as his only compensation. And he was about to lose his health insurance by January 1st, a fact that the Merrill manager forgot to share three weeks earlier when Mike was packing his family photos into a box at his empty office.

On the morning of New Year's Eve, Mike and I rushed to the county insurance office that was closing early at noon. We quickly filled out paperwork to add Mike and the kids to my health insurance provided by the public library. We drove home in silence. I made turkey sandwiches for the children who ate at the table on the back porch. Mike went for a run around the neighborhood. The kids played in the back yard as I sat on the porch's upholstered chaise, my mind racing to think of what jobs could be available for an overqualified fifty-five year old man in a limited market.

Gilly's volleyball club season was about to begin and that meant club fees would be due. Hotels would need to be booked. She needed new shoes for the court. Griffin had just started guitar lessons and he was a natural, fretting the strings like a young Hendrix. He had potential.

I went to bed early. I was not in the mood to celebrate a new year that promised new worries. I woke up in the middle of the night when the noise in my head returned. I couldn't turn it off. I started thinking about bigger ticket items beside volleyball shoes and guitar lessons. Like car payments. And the utility bill. And the mortgage on our house that now had a brass plaque affixed to it.

Mike was sound asleep beside me. I got up and pulled the blanket at the foot of the bed around me like a protective cape. Dragging the blanket down the stairwell, I tip-toed into the library. I ran my fingers along book spines on the Paul Revere Pewter-painted shelves. *The Style Book, Volume One* was on my desk. So was another book, *The Story Pole*, written by one of my most favorite writers of all—Sherman Yeary.

After Dad retired, he signed up for an autobiography writing class through the college's continuing education program. He had always been a voracious reader and now he had time to become a voracious writer. He churned out five self-published books, each about growing up in the small town of Ocala that had then become a nice-sized city. He wrote about his building career, his all-girl family, his grandchildren, his friends, his faith, his community. One book focused on the businesses located around Main and Magnolia Streets, two iconic areas in downtown. Another was dedicated to life and commerce around the city's court house square.

Dad's writings were his homage to home. He became a local celebrity, autographing his soft-cover books at the bookstore, giving copies to the city council and county commission. The newspaper often referenced him as a subject matter expert on Ocala/Marion County history. Dad was in his element. He had found himself.

The Story Pole was his first book. Its white glossy soft-bound cover had two black and white photos of Dad, one as a child and one as an adult, standing next to what looked like a pole hand-drawn in a thin Sharpie felt tip. He introduced his book describing the story pole, made of a tall piece of wood, as one of the most practical and economical tools in the construction industry. He used the story pole as a benchmark for keeping a constant level on his work site. It would top out masonry work, measure window and door heights and check the height of every cement block. Dad wrote that life was a lot like the story pole.

"We all need a benchmark in our life, a point of beginning," Dad wrote,

"Something to keep us level and plumb, to measure our lives by."

Dad had died five years earlier, two days after Christmas, five weeks after my porch party. He'd promised he'd share Christmas with me. Dad always kept his promises. And he made me promise I'd keep writing because he knew how much that meant to the both of us. Writing saved Dad after he had put down his toolbox and fought to stay alive with a fragile heart. He knew what a good story was capable of.

Wrapping the blanket around my shoulders, I turned on the CD player and sat in the recliner where I had placed *The Story Pole* on the seat. Dad's porch party music was playing Sinatra's "Wee Small Hours of the Morning." Thanks, Dad, I thought, as I curled up my knees to my chest and buried my face in the blanket to keep my family from hearing me fall apart. I had to be strong for Griffin and Gilly. For Mike. For Dad.

"The pole says I've lived, had good times, struggles and victories," Dad wrote in his prologue. "I have never traveled too far from the benchmark, from a sixteen penny nail in an old oak tree, a friend or family. I can always go back to my beginnings, to the story pole and remember."

The next morning, I woke up in the recliner, my neck aching from an awkward and restless sleep. The sun filtered through the window blinds like a splintered spotlight on my desk. I returned Dad's book to its usual place next to my laptop computer. I walked upstairs and brushed my teeth and was tempted to crawl back into bed next to Mike and pull the covers over my face until a year or so had gone by and life had gotten level and plumb again.

Instead, I put on my pale pink, soft fleece sweatpants and sweatshirt. I breathed deeply in and out and suited up my emotional armor to face the battle of the unknown.

Continuing to write was the last thing on my mind in spite of the promise I'd made to Dad. And I didn't exactly have a lot of outlets to write for anymore. The housing market was collapsing and taking down everything with it, including magazines and books about houses. Plus, I had a new full-time job outside of the writing world I once inhabited.

Yet an empty corduroy-covered photo album that sat at the bottom of my library's gray-painted bookshelf would soon serve as unexpected poetic permission for me to write again in a way I never had before. But I would not write about elegant and beautiful homes that possessed an innate sense of style. Or of the people who lived in them. Instead, I would eventually write of the one thing I was beginning to fear I could lose, a loss that would be greater than the prospect of leaving Oak Lane Cottage.

Chapter 4

The Family Room: Hell No Haiku

On her dusty coffee table, mom kept an old copy of a city magazine, a wedding-themed issue with a photo of a bride and groom smiling as big as the bride's white tulle veil. The groom, a ringer for a young Tom Selleck with midnight black thick wavy hair and a mustache, gazed intently into the eyes of his blonde bride dressed in pearls, sequins and tulle. Lots of tulle. "The Marriage of Mike and Amy Mangan" was the headline in the center of a pink heart.

I would've scrapped the heart clip art if I were editor. Keep it simple. The inside piece, titled "Doing It Right," was about Ocala's hometown couple who had wanted to create an ideal wedding with their 1990 December nuptials that topped over four hundred in attendance at First Baptist Church of Ocala with a big band reception afterward at a nearby garden club. Maybe the headline should've been "Doing It Big."

Eighteen years later, as an eighty-three-year-old widow, Mom still had the magazine. One day I brought Chinese takeout and the children with me to visit her and said, "Mom, I think we can retire this issue."

I was thumbing through the pages and had stopped on the one with a photo of Dad dressed in a white-tailed tuxedo. He was proudly perched on a church pew, a happy day for him, the last of his girls was married and—remarkably—every one of them lived in Ocala except for his oldest, who lived only forty-five minutes away. Even more remarkable since his youngest daughter had previously declared she would never return to Ocala and never marry anyone from there either.

Never say never.

Cleaning up after dinner while Griffin and Gilly visited with mom, I opened her refrigerator to store the remaining shrimp fried rice and a pungent smell overcame me. I found the culprit, a plastic container of meatloaf gelled over with spongy green mold, dinner from January. It was now the end of February. Next to the meatloaf was a carton of rotten eggs.

Grabbing a trash bag, I dumped out the eggs and meatloaf. Mom's kitchen was cluttered with trash, with dirty dishes in the sink and with far too many prescription bottles on the counter. My sisters and I had tried to talk to mom about selling her house and moving into an assisted living facility, but she wanted no part of it. Scrubbing caked-on food from a fork at the sink, I started to wonder how much longer mom could live here.

Mom had been with Dad for most of her life, meeting him at a church youth group, marrying young, staying at home with her girls while Dad worked in construction. When I was in high school, mom spread her wings and secured her real estate and broker's license. Eventually she had her own realty company. She was a professional success by her late fifties and sold houses until she turned eighty, coming into her own when most women in her generation were collecting social security. And she thrived, creating her own network of work friends and associates.

By then, however, she was also a full-time caregiver to her ailing husband, another role she embraced with grace and acceptance—so much that a big black hole was left in her life when Dad died. Her care-giving job had ended and age and health now kept her from staying in real estate even though she kept her license with a local and kind realtor. She was not safe driving on the road, yet another battle my sisters and I continued to lose. One night she ended up in my driveway at Oak Lane, her car still running with the driver's side door open, while she rang my doorbell frantically asking if I could tell her how to get to the house where her company's Christmas party was being held, a place she had frequently visited.

Cleaning up her kitchen, I dreaded the inevitable task of uprooting mom's life and could not address it at that moment. It was a school night for Griffin and Gilly and a work night for me so we kissed mom good night.

Gilly was holding the wedding magazine as she got into the car.

"Mamaw said I could have it," Gilly said. "You were so pretty, Mama."

Pretty naïve, I thought, as I pulled out of mom's driveway. The bride on the magazine cover was possessed with a great deal of youthful optimism about life and marriage. Look at her, I thought, beaming into the eyes of her new husband, proud of pulling off a well-planned wedding extravaganza. I had spent a month's paycheck on that bridal gown and the crystal and tulle headpiece cost extra.

And look at me now.

I peered into the rearview mirror and saw a woman with raccoon circles beneath her eyes, consumed by doubt about whether she could manage to keep her family afloat. Eighteen years earlier, my biggest concern had been whether to have a sit-down dinner or a buffet-style meal for my wedding guests. Tonight, I hoped my $22 splurge on Chinese takeout hadn't left me with an overdrawn checking account.

Back home, after homework was done, the children joined me on the couch in front of the TV in the family room, a cozy space with a bright yellow-red-and-green plaid sofa and love seat centered near a forest green leather ottoman, the only customized furniture I had ever splurged on. I chose the bright and multi-colored fabric for the couches and Mike picked the more conservative dark-hued leather for the ottoman.

I once wrote in a home makeover story that the family room was the heart of the home. Ours was no exception with its side door entrance at one end of the room and our famous porch, connected by a large paned window, on the other so it got a lot of foot traffic. The family room was bathed in a warm tan brick on the floor and the fireplace. To complement the light stone, I painted the paneled walls "Relaxed Khaki" from Sherwin Williams.

Mike was working the second shift, three p.m. to midnight, at a call center, as he had done for the past two months since losing his Merrill Lynch job. I tried to avoid watching mindless television shows as our nightly escape while Mike sat across town in a cubicle cold-calling people to buy magazine subscriptions.

Our new evening routine without Mike took some getting used to. We wanted the old routine back when Mike was home at night and would peel a Granny Smith apple after dinner and share it with the kids as we piled close together on the couch, feet propped up on the ottoman in front of the fireplace. Sometimes we'd make s'mores with burnt marshmallows pierced on coat hanger rods dangling over the fire as Honey anxiously sat close by, hoping for an errant melted marshmallow to come her way. I missed that. And our dinners together in the dining room where we would recount the events of the day, almost competing for air time because we all had so much to say. And our frequent post-bath evening ritual where we'd relax onto the back porch chaises. And fall asleep in our adjoining upstairs bedrooms as Gilly's stereo played James Taylor's *October Road* album, filtering his silky serenade through our hallway.

And I missed escaping at night to my library to read and write. Now I sat in front of the laptop at my desk searching for jobs for Mike, printing ones with potential which Mike often ignored. At first, I rationalized Mike's tepid response. He was emotionally drained from our chaotic job losses, hesitant to make another career move, fearful it could be a wrong one. Always cautious and methodical,

Mike did not jump into anything. Crawling may have even been an exaggeration for his approach. For years before leaving the insurance agency, he had researched his exit options, writing out his plan on a yellow legal size notepad. Then he'd research further and crunch more numbers. He did not rush in where angels feared to tread. He'd be the guy behind the angels shaking his head saying, "Uh-huh, this definitely requires further analysis. Let me get out my notepad."

Mike believed he had taken the appropriate steps to find the right career. Now he was taking subscription orders by phone. And I was home trying to maintain a sense of normalcy for Griffin and Gillian.

That night, we'd exhausted playing all of our board games and no one felt like playing cards. Sometimes we'd read, so I pulled a children's poetry collection off the library shelf. Poetry wasn't a usual family go-to, but on that night it was. I returned to the family room where the children and I took turns reading a few poems, including William Carlos Williams's *The Red Wheelbarrow*.

Surprisingly, reading about a metaphoric piece of garden equipment calmed us. So much, that we shared reading aloud other poems. I saw a light in Griffin and Gilly's eyes. They were such good troopers, adjusting to their parents' new work realities and going along with Mama's spontaneous evening family activities. I didn't take for granted that I had terrific kids who could've been sulking, narcissistic adolescents hiding in their bedrooms playing video games. Instead, they were sitting on the ottoman waiting for another poem. I didn't want to let them down. Much of our future seemed out of my control, yet this much I could do: love them and be present.

I walked into the adjoining kitchen and pulled out a handful of small note cards and ink pens from a drawer. Hey, if a wheelbarrow could be a source of poetic inspiration, maybe other things could be, too.

Back in the family room, we wrote poems about anything and everything, mainly what was right in front of us. We wrote about the television, our tennis shoes, the water pitcher, the dog, even a portrait of me as a young girl. Gilly deemed my eyes in the pencil sketch to be like "saltwater." I wasn't sure what that meant, but loved it just the same. Our humble verses were concise enough to fit on a note card. Another William Carlos Williams poem, "Perfection," inspired us. Williams wrote of a shriveled apple that remained lovely in the eyes of the writer. Griffin penned his thoughts about a decorative box next to our fireplace.

"Many mistake it for ugly
But I have seen its inner self
A few years ago it sat there in a market

Waiting to be bought
Waiting to be used for the first time
Waiting for me to come and see its true beauty."
Gilly was up next, choosing her shoe as her poetic muse.
"From new to old
It does not shine anymore
The tennis shoe glimmered once
Even in the mud
And it told a story of how it helped me
Running in the rain."

We wrote a few nights each week. Months passed and we had created quite a nice poetry collection. Originally I kept the note cards in a basket, but, afraid they'd get tossed out, I grabbed an empty black corduroy photo album to store the cards in its plastic sleeves. We called our book the *Oak Lane Cottage Anthology of Random Poetry.*

On the rare nights he was home, Mike joined our poetry sessions, but usually bowed out after a few minutes. He'd beg off by saying he wanted to get a run in before it turned dark. Or he needed to use the bathroom, which often became a prolonged stay. I knew I wouldn't see him for a while when he took a sports magazine in with him.

Despite understanding that Mike needed downtime, I came to resent his choices. He'd take a nap when he should've been helping Gilly practice volleyball. He'd go for a long run in the neighborhood instead of listening to Griffin play the guitar. And he'd head to the bathroom for an epic who-knows-what session when he should've been with me figuring out how we were going to keep our house and family together.

Mike came into the kitchen after one early evening run, enjoying a rare night off from working at the call center. The kids and I were at the kitchen island pasting photos and printed graphs on a large tri-fold poster board for Griffin's science project. I was a science project veteran who knew Super Glue was the answer to almost everything, including eye-catching posters with pictures that wouldn't fall off. We were carefully positioning our art on the board. Once you Super Glued, you were committed.

"Hey, I need to chat with you," I said to Mike as he poured water from the sink's faucet into a glass. I motioned to the back porch and left the Super Glue duties to Griffin.

"Ok, let me take a shower first," he said.

"We really need to talk," I said without giving him an option as I opened the door to the porch where we could talk in private.

"Gilly's club volleyball tuition is due," I said, "I've already bartered some of it in exchange for writing the club's newsletter, but we've got to pay the rest of it."

"I know," Mike said. "That's why I'm working to find another job as fast as I can."

"Well, I think you could work a little harder at that," I said tersely.

"Oh, come on," Mike shook his head, "Honey, we're in the middle of a historic economic collapse. There aren't a lot of jobs out there right now."

"Well, I've managed to find a few for you online while I'm also working and taking care of the kids," I said. "If you have time to go for a run, you have time to look for a job."

"I do look! And don't give me that! Running helps me stay healthy and blow off steam. I've told you I wish you would do the same. It would be good for you," Mike snapped. "And most of those jobs you've shown me aren't realistic. Are we going to move to another city?"

"I don't know, Mike," I said, "I actually don't know what we are going to do because you won't talk to me about it."

"Yes, I have," Mike walked past me. "And we will figure this out. I'm going to take a shower so I can be with the kids before they go to bed."

The porch turned dark and quiet like the night's cold winter air. I pulled my nubby wool sweater more closely around me, soaking in the frigid unsolicited solitude until a yelp came from the kitchen.

"Gilly!" Griffin yelled. "Look what you did!"

I returned inside to see an upside down pie chart Super Glued in the middle of Griffin's poster board. Gilly was trying to help her big brother, not realizing he had already applied glue to the paper, and she had placed it on the board to see if it looked good in that spot. They both started to cry.

"It's okay. We can print another chart and glue it on top and you won't even see it," I said. We fixed the upside-down picture while Mike took a shower. Later, when he came downstairs, the science project was finished and so was I.

"Glad you could join us, we're done," I said. "I'm going to look for more jobs on the computer."

I started keeping score every time Mike wasn't with us when I thought he should be. I knew better, knew no one wins with emotionally charged mental tallying, but this is what happens when fear replaces certainty. The scorecard comes out. Disappointment. Check. Anger. Check. Resentment. Big check. I was deep-boned scared of the unknown, gun shy from all that had happened to us in the past eight months.

And I was alone, drafting out a three-month plan for our finances, for our future. And Mike, carrying the weight of our mercurial circumstances on his hunched-down broad shoulders, had relegated his yellow legal notepad to his desk drawer in our bedroom.

But I always had a plan, like an appendage to my body. Mike used to joke about our engagement that he thought he had a little more time before getting married after proposing to me on a trip to San Francisco, but his new fiancée had whipped out her calendar planner on the airplane and circled a wedding date six months later. Sometimes I wondered if I hadn't circled that date, if we had waited to get married, if we had waited on Mike, would we have ended up together?

When the shadows came, doubt entered, too. As unproductive and dangerous as it was, I questioned everything about my life. Why did I leave my secure teaching job for a far-flung notion I could make it as a writer? Why did Mike wait so long, maybe too long, to leave the insurance agency to find a better job? When I really wanted to drive myself insane, I'd flip my mental rationale and wonder why Mike didn't work harder to make the insurance agency more successful. And why didn't I finish my doctorate and become a college president?

Such were the questions of a mad woman surrounded by debt and worry. And Mike's bathroom obsession had driven me mad.

Once, he was in there so long that I slipped copies of job applications beneath the lit bathroom door while the kids and I sat on the floor on the other side. It was our Occupy the Bathroom. It became a battle of wills. He wouldn't come out. Grif and Gilly wrote notes and pushed them underneath the door.

"I'll be out in a minute," Mike said angrily.

"You've been in there forever!" Gilly yelled into the door.

We pounded our fists to the floor chanting, "We want Mike! We want Mike!" and started laughing until it wasn't funny anymore. He wasn't budging.

"Come on, kids, let's make chocolate chip cookies," I said, standing up to head into the kitchen.

Mike and I went to bed in sullen contempt that night, something I swore I wouldn't do in my marriage. "Never go to bed angry," my mom would say. I broke other vows, too, like pitting the kids against my husband. Using them to get Mike's attention was low, like reality show low. I despised hearing of women who used their children as ploys to motivate their husbands no matter the cause. Children shouldn't be pawns. Griffin and Gilly didn't create the dire financial situation we were in. We did. So did John Thain. I liked to personally blame the former Merrill Lynch CEO who finally resigned after his Christmas executive bonus controversy. But Thain landed on his feet, snagging another multimillion dollar corporate contract, a fitting reward for poor performance.

My mother also said, "When money troubles come through the front door, love goes out the window," an odd quote from someone who was happily married for over fifty years, but I got the drift. When money troubles walked into our home, Mike walked into the bathroom. And I got petty and resentful...of a toilet.

Mike and I approached our crisis from different perspectives. We always had. I was the take-charge and Mike was the take-time to figure out a problem. That's what had made our relationship exciting and fresh when we were first together. Opposites attract and, in many ways, we were as different as night and day. Mike was health-conscious. If he was stressed, he went for a run. I was usually hungry. When pressure mounted, I went for a chocolate bar. Mike had a small circle of friends. My social net was broader. Some would say he was the introvert and I, the extrovert. But we were both introverted, I just responded to life differently.

That didn't mean I had to take on the world when necessary, quite the opposite. I also wanted to go inside, retreat for a little while. I had always needed my own space, internally and emotionally, to recharge my batteries. I, too, wanted my own toilet where I could close the door and hide. But one of us had to face the world at the present moment. And that appeared to be me. I didn't remember voting on that decision. Mike was known for being quiet and contemplative, but his job loss and our mounting financial troubles made him catatonic.

I had to find another way to work through our issues. Therapy wasn't an option—too expensive. Wine was a consideration, but it gave me a headache. Vodka often helped. Then I discovered an outlet cheaper than both a counselor and alcohol and it came in the form of a three by five-sized note card. I sorted out my anger and frustration during poetry nights with the kids, only they didn't know. While they wrote haikus about the moon and the dog, I wrote about Mike.

"He sits on his throne
Sitting and reading alone
While our world crumbles"

I saved these verses along with a handful of others, tucked away in the bottom drawer of my bedside stand. Some nights, when I couldn't sleep, I took a blank note card from the drawer and added another hell no haiku to my private collection.

By late spring, Mike found a job as a loan officer at a bank. All of my caution alarms were going off. Banks were in trouble. The federal government was stepping in and, apparently, so was Mike. Most people run from a fire, not into it. Had Mike been sleeping under a rock or had he just spent too much time in the bathroom?

For months I tried to steer Mike in another direction, any direction, away from the unstable financial world, but he wouldn't have it. He was hell bent on proving this is where he should be. It was his wheelhouse. He was good at it. He passed his securities brokers license the first time, remember?

We had reached a marital impasse. While his new position afforded much needed stability and income, I had come to believe it may have been too little, too late. We were behind in our monthly mortgage payment. And car payment. We were behind in almost everything. The daily mail greeted us with more bills, more past-due reminders.

"We got another notice from the mortgage company," I said, tossing the certified letter across our bed as Mike sat on the edge of it, pulling off his work shoes.

"I'll call them on my lunch break tomorrow," he said, not looking up.

"A lot of good that will do," I said. "We might as well list the house before we lose it."

"I don't want it to come to that, but maybe it wouldn't hurt to talk to the realtor," Mike said and wadded up his worn socks to throw into the closet's laundry basket. "I'm going to change clothes and take Gilly to volleyball practice."

Mike wasn't working the call center night shift anymore so we could return to a somewhat normal schedule, though it didn't matter. We had retreated into our respective corners, coming out only to be with the children. That much we still shared in common, both fiercely loyal to Griffin and Gilly. I preferred their company over anyone's. Our poetry nights were welcome pockets of relief.

One night the children and I sat in the family room while Mike went for a long run. It was haiku night again. Griffin read his verse called "Waiting."

"Mother nature's child
Sits in the meadow of peace
Waiting for the green"

I looked at my teenage boy, a spitting youthful image of Mike. Griffin had his father's dark Irish looks, thick jet black hair, olive skin and deep-set eyes. Handsome, but unaware of it, just like Mike, who wasn't vain and ever shunned the spotlight, a trait I loved about him when we had dated.

Now he was shunning the most important people in his life. And I couldn't fix him.

Watching Griffin read his haiku, I wondered what the future had in store for him. He was on the cusp of so much. He was a lot like Mike—quiet, whip smart, self-effacing. He was like me as well, interested in a variety of subjects from history to politics, even at his young age. He could be stubborn, too, a genetic gift from both strong-willed parents. But I hoped it would help him in a good way. Grif would need a healthy reserve of confidence heading into the brutal turf of high school. Would our unsteady lives undermine him?

I closed my eyes for a minute to keep from crying. I wanted my own meadow of peace. I wanted my marriage to be what I thought it would be when I wore five pounds of tulle on my head at the wedding of doing-things-right. I wanted Mike to fight for us. I wanted him to hold my hand and tell me we'd get through this rough time together because that's who we were. We were partners. We were fighters. We wouldn't quit.

I went upstairs to my bedside table, opened the bottom drawer and read the cards that no one else would see. The signs were all there. How did I not see them earlier?

Then, in August, we were forced to place a new sign in our front yard, one that Mike and I could no longer ignore.

House For Sale.

Chapter 5

The Foyer: The Umbrella Stand

In spite of a volatile housing market, I had no doubt Oak Lane would sell quickly. One step inside the foyer would seal the deal. It had for me.

When the realtor first showed us the house, I envisioned my decorating plans the minute I laid eyes on the brick steps leading up to a paneled door, which I soon replaced with a glass French door. Light-colored bricks, almost taupe in shade, framed the four front windows and door. Once we bought it, I painted the shutters and door in a creamy beige to compliment the brick. Mike added a picket fence, painted with the same color. Very creamy dreamy. It looked like a muted Thomas Kinkaid painting minus the glistening snow, illuminated streams and Bible verses.

Inside the foyer I placed a black-lacquered side table next to the stairwell and hung a large mirror over the table that held various accessories, depending on the season. Springtime invited my ceramic pastel eggs and rabbit figurines to be displayed on the table by a candy dish of jellybeans. Christmas? Pinecones and framed holiday photos. My favorite season was fall, when I'd bring out the miniature wooden pumpkins with pumpkin shaped candies in the multi-seasonal candy dish next to a pumpkin scented candle because I ascribed to the Pier One belief that you really can't have too much pumpkin.

I had painted the entryway walls in a muted mossy green that subtly reflected the warmth of our newly-installed wood floors. However, there wasn't a cover over the entry. That didn't bother me until it would rain and guests would either walk in wet or—horrors!—choose the *other* front entrance, a door with a porch overhang next to the street-facing a double garage, thereby missing my foyer with thematic décor rivaling a Macy's window in New York City. I needed a solution that didn't break the bank or require a structural addition.

One day, the month before I lost my job at the magazine, I was at a furniture consignment store shopping for photo shoot props for a home makeover story I was producing. I saw a vintage hammered brass stand in the shape of an umbrella on a circular base. The stand was designed with the umbrella open upside down, as if it had been left it in a corner to dry. The curved handle was on top, leaving space for real umbrellas to be deposited in the stand. Voila! Problem solved! And it was twenty-five dollars. Cheap and efficient! I picked it up and headed to the cashier.

Then I stopped. I looked at the stand again. Did I really need a hammered brass umbrella stand? Our foyer had a coat closet beneath the stairwell that could easily serve as an umbrella depository.

Hesitantly, I put the stand back.

But the next week, I thought about the umbrella stand again and returned to the store for a few quick visits. The store owner was losing his patience. He kept giving me a look like, *Just buy the damn thing.* Each time, I left empty-handed.

What's odd about the umbrella dilemma of 2008 is that I was normally a very decisive person, not one to hesitate or second guess, especially on something as trivial as a home accessory purchase. I soon realized the umbrella stand was a distraction from a different storm that was brewing and about to reach our home.

Oak Lane sold within sixty days. The buyers liked my foyer, too, and the rest of the house, especially the back porch, and they bought everything from it down to the curtains. We had to be out by early November. I hoped we could have one last Thanksgiving there, but knew better than to push my luck as the housing market was crashing around me. We found a three-bedroom apartment in the children's school district, but it wouldn't be ready until December, so we planned to move into a furnished two-bedroom in the same complex for a few weeks. The apartments were temporary, I assured the children. Soon, we would find a new home, I told them and hoped that would be true.

Mike and I put aside our differences and focused on the move. It was important to us both to make this transition as easy as possible for Griffin and Gilly. They'd already been through enough with their parents' rotating jobs. And I had just accepted another one. One of the city magazines had suddenly lost their editor and called me with an offer I couldn't refuse—better salary, flexibility to be home when the kids were home and a return to a profession that I loved and missed. The public library had been so good to me, but I had to scratch this creative itch once more.

We pared down our stuff significantly to host a mother-of-all-garage sales. No wobbly card tables in a garage for us. We were selling most of the contents in our home so we opened up the house and let people come in so they could shop room by room. Then we packed up the things that we'd bring to the apartment and the other large items we planned to keep, like our dining room table and chairs, but would put in the storage unit beneath our second-floor apartment.

I didn't stop to think about what I was losing because I didn't have time to. That's what I said to friends when they delivered take-out Thai dinner or helped me pack my china and crystal in bubble wrap. Each time I greeted a friend into our foyer, I hugged them longer than usual. It was a goodbye more than hello and we both knew it. Oak Lane was special. It was our forever home until it couldn't be that anymore, so we reminisced about the memories and parties and dinners and porch nights and martinis—yes, especially the martinis—we had shared there. Yet, it was the season of Thanksgiving and I had much for which to be thankful. We sold our house, we didn't lose it. We both had jobs. Our children were healthy.

I was deeply grateful to my friends and sisters. They showed up. They packed. They brought pans of lasagna and brownies in disposable dishes. They questioned, but did not argue about why I was keeping the extra set of "good china" that Mike's grandmother once owned. They helped me polish off the chilled champagne I'd forgotten about in the back of the refrigerator. They also commiserated with me about John Thain, that son-of-a-bitch mega-millionaire, rolling in his millions while many of his former employees rolled up the welcome mats to their homes. This was totally misplaced, pent-up anger, but that's what friends are for when the clouds appear—to validate misplaced, pent-up anger, at least for a little while. I needed them to say, "You're right, this sucks. John Thain sucks." And they did, God bless them.

Speaking of John Thain, turns out he had something of a decorating bug himself, spending over one million company dollars to renovate his corporate office the year before the merger. The same year Merrill bled twenty-seven billion dollars in losses.

$87,784 for a rug.

$68,179 for a credenza.

$1,405 for a parchment waste can.

His curtains alone cost $28,091.

Just to name a few items.

This on top of the bonus payments that were moved to December, right before shareholders approved the merger, instead of the usual time in January. Some received hundreds of millions in bonuses while Mike—who annually made less than Thain's office rug purchase—received his two-week notice.

Thain's conspicuous and extravagant office expenses inspired comparisons to other corporate execs, namely Dennis Kozlowski, the former CEO of Tyco International, who was convicted of defrauding shareholders of millions of dollars and handing out more than one hundred and fifty million dollars in bonuses. His expenditures included a fifteen thousand dollar umbrella stand shaped like a poodle. The owner of the shop who sold Kozlowski the umbrella stand got testy when reporters called.

"It's not just some stupid umbrella stand," the store owner said, "It's a very unique, beautiful piece."

November, the season of thanks, became our shedding season. We were quickly learning to be experts in the field of paring down things and expectations and deleting a few dreams even. One, in particular. We would not grow old in Oak Lane Cottage.

The night before the moving truck arrived to take what was left of our belongings, we ate cheese pizza on paper plates in our dining room. Gilly looked around the room that was now empty except for the table and chairs.

"Mama, did we sell the candle sconces?" she asked, ever my decorating buddy.

"No, sweetie, those will be kept in the apartment's storage unit," I said, remembering when we first moved into Oak Lane and Gilly and I spray painted rust-colored sconces a glossy white, before hanging them on the dining room wall that was painted an olive green. We were quite proud of our finished product.

"What about the mirror that used to be here?" Gilly asked pointing to the side wall.

"Um, we sold it in the garage sale," I said.

"I liked that mirror," Gilly replied.

"I did, too," Griffin said.

"We've had a lot of great memories in this room and this house," Mike added, turning to me.

That's when it hit me. I couldn't look at him. We were really leaving Oak Lane.

I had been so busy packing and selling and getting the house in order that I hadn't allowed myself time to stop and think about what was actually happening, but I didn't want our last night there to get lost in the moving frenzy. It mattered to me that the children left our home grateful for what we once had, not what we were losing. I was glad we had come together, if only for an hour's respite over greasy cheese pizza.

For the next few minutes, we shared our favorite Oak Lane memories. I sat at one end of the table facing the foyer. We used to joke it was our foyer dance floor because we'd usually end up dancing there after dinner, Mike with Gilly and Griffin with me, swaying closely in the small entryway to the quiet jazz of John Coltrane and Chet Baker playing on the stereo in the nearby library.

"I'll miss our foyer dance floor," I said, welling up with tears that I dabbed off my cheek with a paper napkin. Mike reached for my arm, but I pulled away. If he touched me, it would dislodge the grief that was sitting in my chest, bubbling to the surface, about to spill out into uncontrollable sadness. *It's just a house, it's just a house*, I kept telling myself, chanting like an exiled Tibetan monk.

When we were first married, Mike and I had had dreams about how our lives would turn out. What we hoped to accomplish, the kind of family we would raise, the home we would live in and fill with memories and traditions and love.

But, we would not fill Oak Lane's foyer anymore with wooden pumpkins and scented pinecones and rabbit figurines. Or an upside down umbrella stand that, at one time, seemed most beautiful and unique to me.

PART TWO: THE APARTMENT

Chapter 6

The Kitchen: Dreaming of Italy

When I woke the first morning in our temporary furnished apartment, the complex's model unit, my head was pounding so badly I couldn't see clearly. As my head pulsated with an electric drum in the center of my forehead, I reached from my bed toward the bedside chest of drawers where I kept my migraine medicine and reading glasses. A faint morning light slivered through floor-length curtains and I patted my hand up and down the side of the drawers like an aimless mime.

A few minutes of this continued before I remembered that my mother's antique bedside table—the one that had been by every bed I had ever slept in and was where I kept my glasses, medicine and miniature reading light—was in the storage unit beneath the apartment we had rented, but which would only be ready two weeks later after the current tenants had moved out. Most of our stuff was still packed and duck-taped in boxes next to my missing bedside table.

We had only brought clothes and essentials to our model unit called "The Wellington," a royal-sounding floor-plan for an apartment more fitting for the downstairs help than for the Duke of Wellington. It had chipped Formica bathroom countertops, a cheap piled carpet that snagged on my heels and a stupid-ass bedside table without drawers. The apartment complex's general manager said we were lucky to get this unit. The only other temporary model— the one called "The Cambridge"—had "some issues."

Sliding out of bed, I found my white robe and two mismatched red and yellow nubby socks in my suitcase. When I reached the tiny kitchen—which took about two seconds—my headache had reached a new crescendo of ice-pick pain. The kitchen reeked of bleach, vinegar and citrus spray that made me lightheaded as I opened the refrigerator's freezer door. Still no sign of my medicine on the adjoining kitchen counter. Did I accidentally pack it in the storage unit?

I gently grabbed a few ice cubes—even the sound of shifting ice hurt my head—and wrapped them in a dishtowel that I planned to put on my forehead once I laid on the couch in the family room that was connected to the kitchen. But before I got that far, a volcanic wave of nausea hit me in perfect bitter-tasting tempo with the staccato drumming in my head. I leaned into the kitchen sink trying to hold back the leftover pizza I had brought from the house and had eaten the night before—something that suddenly seemed like a very bad decision. If I moved, I feared I would faint. So I slowly tilted my head, left ear down, on the kitchen counter to slide the iced towel over between my eyes.

I was relieved Mike had already taken the children to school. I wouldn't have wanted them, on the first morning in their new place, to walk in the kitchen and see their mother splayed out on the floor, red and yellow socks and all. He had packed their lunches, too. I meant to wake up early and make our favorite sour cream banana pancakes and over-easy eggs as reassurance this new chapter in our lives would be just fine because we had each other and homemade pancakes and The Wellington model unit. Lucky us. But, they were gone. I had missed my chance to make their first breakfast here a familiar and pleasant one. I bent over into the sink hurling the last meal I had at Oak Lane.

Welcome Home.

·   ·   ·   ·   ·   ·

It was final proofs week at the magazine and I was on a tight deadline to make the last edits to the red-lined book which wasn't a book, but an oversized four-color copy of the monthly publication. My new job was not what I had hoped. The erratic management and pay added to the chaos of the undisciplined work environment.

Before my unwelcome encounter with the kitchen sink, I'd hoped to edit the book in the apartment. I worked better in a quiet environment and my third-floor office at the publishing company was anything but calm, the "third-floor" being a euphemism for a cramped attic in a historic house on the edge of the city's business district where two editors, the creative director and a student intern crowded together over used furniture shoved together as work desks. I'd already lost my early morning proofing with the headache that wouldn't go away. My doctor's office said they could squeeze me in if I could make it before noon.

I can make it there in ten minutes, I said.

Drawing a fat bell curve on his prescription pad, my doctor, sitting on a stool by my chair in the patient's room, announced my prognosis. I was entering menopause. Here's where you are, he said, pointing to the first part of the curve. Here's where you will be in a few years. He traced his black-ink pen over the mountain-like slope that dropped down to a flat line.

"This explains the migraines," I said, adding I never even had an aspirin-worthy headache until my forties.

"This explains the migraines," he echoed. Then he jotted out a prescription for a triptan and talked about healthy lifestyles for women going through menopause. Exercise. Diet. Importance of calcium, like celebrity actresses endorse on commercials. Rest. And managing stress.

I looked down at my lap on that last one.

"Amy, I don't think the migraines are just because you're beginning menopause," he said, placing his pen on the counter and looking directly toward me with a crooked smile. "I know you and Mike have been through a lot lately."

There it was. Small town living in high-def. Everyone knew everyone's business, mine included.

My heart began to race with a warm rush to my chest. I didn't know what to say, embarrassed that my doctor, a very busy and successful professional with a standing-room-only waiting room of patients, was not so busy that it prevented him from knowing about the recent trials of the Mangan family. My Southern Protestant upbringing—a double whammy of compassion and judgment—shaped my sensibilities about intimacy. I was raised to know it was good to share with others about my faith, my dreams, my recipe for a killer mac and cheese.

But the real stuff? Like money and marriage troubles? Folks would scurry like cockroaches when the lights came on if I brought up that Mike and I had a hundred dollars to get us through the next two weeks and that we barely spoke except for talking about the children and mounting debt. And my job was a train wreck. There was that, too. No one would want to know that, I thought.

"Oh, we're fine," I said, smiling like Best Actress in a Lead Role, "Just going through a few speed bumps."

My doctor nodded.

"Well, it's important to find healthy ways to relieve stress and that will help minimize your migraines," he said and give me a knowing grin with perfectly capped teeth, like white Lego bricks.

Doctor, that prescription in your hand is going to help me relieve stress, I thought, and wonder how quickly we could wrap up this uninvited therapy session. I picked up my purse as my exit cue.

"You know, my wife was going through a stressful time recently," he said, clearly not ready to end our chat. Didn't this man have fifty other patients waiting to see him?

"I could tell she needed a break," he continued, oblivious to my discomfort.

Oh no, I thought. Please, let's not discuss your stay-at-home well-toned country club wife.

"She was so frazzled with the kids and their school activities and her volunteer work that I sent her and a friend to Italy this week just to get away," my thoughtful doctor said, shoulders bowed up in his white coat, proud of his benevolent gesture.

"They are going to Rome and Venice," he added, "And I'm leaving early each day to pick up the kids."

Well, aren't you the Millionaire Husband of the Year, I wanted to say, but resisted because the migraine prescription was just within my reach. I muttered something like good for you, grabbed the script and got the hell out of there.

Now, past one o'clock without lunch or a magazine proof, I stopped by the grocery store to grab a deli sandwich and pick up fresh fruit to go with the pancakes that, come hell, high water or headache, I would make for the children the next morning. The kids would love shrimp scampi for dinner, too, but shrimp was expensive, so spaghetti and meat sauce that was buy one-get one free would be our evening meal.

In the deli line I bumped into a woman I casually knew. Dressed in a bright lime-green tennis outfit with highlighted hair pulled into a ponytail beneath a white visor, she was in line behind me. She was picking up a lunch tray for her children's classroom party because she "simply had no time to make anything." She was waving her slender tanned arm, adorned with a sparkling diamond tennis bracelet, while exclaiming to me the plight of the overworked tennis mom. I nodded my head, trying to focus on whether I should order a roast beef sandwich or go with my usual Cuban sub that I could cut in half and save the rest for tomorrow's lunch. She kept talking, rattling on about how busy she was. This must be National Day of Stressed Out Country Club Moms, I thought. Maybe she should visit Italy.

Then she placed her hand on my arm. Instantly, I knew what would come next. I could see it in her face, a look similar to that of my doctor's the moment he'd realized I'd gone through a few changes. From that awkward space, I knew, there would now come an insatiable pursuit on this lime green lady's part of wanting to know more. To know why. To know the gritty details of the Mangan story.

"Hey, I heard you guys moved again."

"Yep. So, have you ever tried the roast beef here?" I pulled my arm away from hers.

"Where did you move to?" she asked, leaning toward me.

"Into an apartment. I've tried their ham, but never the roast beef."

"Really? Wow. Are you going to build or buy?"

"Um, not sure. Hey, do you want to get in front of me to pick up your tray? I know you are busy."

"No, that's fine. Eric told me about Mike's job at Merrill. I can't believe it. He's with the bank now, right?"

"Yeah, it was a shock, but he's happy to have found something else," I replied, now leaning over the deli case and studying the twenty varieties of roast beef with the intensity of a neurosurgeon.

"Are you still writing for the magazine? I can't keep up with how many jobs you've had! How have your kids handled this? But, you've always tried new things. I told Eric he'd have to carry me out of our house even though he wants to move to a smaller house. Who needs six bedrooms, he says to me."

"Yes, I'm writing for the magazine," I said.

My kids are amazingly resilient so I need to be, too, I thought, but did not say.

I like to try new cooking recipes. And reading new authors. And taking family trips even if it is a weekend to the beach, but uprooting my family and life and living in fear if we would have enough money to cover this month's rent was not on my list of new things to try. The *only* thing I really wanted to try right then was to stop answering any more questions about my life. Just let me order the damn roast beef.

That's what I wanted to say. And I wanted to slap her, one of those reality television slaps—arms flailing—where host Andy Cohen steps in and breaks up the scuffle. But I gave her a few more clipped responses, picked up my sandwich and headed to my attic office where I was past deadline with my proof with two hours left to work before I got into the school pick-up car line. I could have asked a friend to pick up Griffin and Gilly, but I'd already missed seeing them that morning. I would finish up the edits at the apartment while they did homework at the kitchen table. Normalcy and routine for the kids drove every decision I made.

Driving to the office, I thought about my doctor and tennis deli line buddy. Pulling into the office parking lot, I sat in the driver's seat preoccupied by who else knew of our problems. Mike and I may have been a hot mess inside, but we were fiercely unified outwardly as a couple who gets through things. Was our veneer chipping, I wondered? A week earlier, a friend who usually never pried had asked me how Mike and I were holding up "as a couple." I'd gone solo to a few public events. And a community leader whom I had interviewed for his bank's advertorial broached the subject of how hard "money issues" are on families. Later, he asked about Mike. A coincidence?

Anxiety intensifies doubt. It was like I had a "We're Screwed" written in black Sharpie on my forehead. I nibbled half of my sandwich like a skittish gerbil before turning off the car to head into my attic workspace.

Later, while waiting in the car line, I thought of how, when the children were little and would get upset, I'd tell them to take a mental time out, like counting to ten or walking away and focusing on something else. As they got older, I'd use my motherly advice to tell them to keep whatever was bothering them in perspective. "In the grand scheme of things, this isn't a big deal." I said that to them so often that I only had to respond with "In the grand scheme of things" and they'd nod their heads.

In the grand scheme of things...

It wasn't cancer.

It wasn't life-threatening.

It wasn't going to permanently alter life as we knew it.

This was small potatoes. I used this one a lot because I liked food.

The Mangan story, which was apparently the emerging topic du jour of our town, was layered with a grand scheme narrative. And, generally, it worked. Life could've been harder with problems we couldn't fix, though we would come to encounter a few of those soon. Mike, Griffin, Gillian and I realized the road could be bumpier in the grand scheme of things. But damn, it sucked sometimes. I also told my children not to say "suck." Life has a way of changing the vernacular of parental guidance.

Leaving Oak Lane and the secure jobs we loved, well, that was tough enough. But having to tell and re-tell the reasons why? Gut-wrenching. I hadn't prepared for this. And I wasn't sure which was worse—facing insensitive people or dealing with those who went radio silent. I wanted it both ways. Don't push me, but don't forget me.

And there were those who forgot. Like Mike's co-workers who felt badly for him, but awkwardly relieved for themselves that they hadn't lost their jobs. I got it. Call anyway. A few did. Well, one actually, who along with his family remained a stalwart friend who gave us grace beyond measure, his wife showing up with a pot of lasagna and homemade brownies the night of Mike's dismissal. And they appeared unannounced on our last day at Oak Lane, ready to help pack as the moving trucks pulled in. They didn't forget.

Nor my friend who greeted me at my apartment door as we were unloading suitcases and dropped off a basket of homemade bran and raisin muffins.

I also encouraged my children not to keep grudges. Keeping score is a metastasized anger that leaves little hope for an emotional cure, I'd tell them, but I was beginning to realize I had fallen into the do-as-I-say-not-as-I-do category with that one. It wasn't so much that I harbored ill will toward those who had hurt or disappointed me in some way, real or perceived. I learned to move on. But, hurt my husband? My kids? The deal was off.

I loved the story from Rabbi Marc Gellman who showed children in his temple a hands-on demonstration of grudge-holding and forgiveness. He hammered nails into a board and told them to think of each nail as a bad thing someone does to another person. With each pounding, the kids got upset. Then he pulled out the nails, asking his young audience to think of that as what happens when we say we're sorry for each bad thing we've done. The children smiled, realizing there is something they could do to make things right. Then he showed them the board with all the nail holes in it. How to get rid of the holes?

They had no idea. He admitted he didn't either. The holes would always be there.

I was trying to hammer fewer holes. I kept the grudge tool kit away from view and tried to remember where I had put my compassion supplies, but sometimes I forgot. It was easier to grimace and grudge. And think about a stressed out doctor's wife touring the Roman ruins. Or a former Merrill Lynch co-worker deleting Mike's cell number.

As the kids piled into the backseat, I made a mental note to do better, fret less and judge little. I was losing my appetite for such pettiness, both in others and in me. Stop thinking about who knows what about us. Who cares? They had holes of their own, often irreparable voids from a tragedy or illness or loss of some kind.

Our afternoon evaporated into early evening at The Wellington. Mike came home before dinner, but I would not tell him that night about my doctor's observation. Or Miss Tennis Bracelet's conversation. While not bred a Protestant, he was raised by an equally stoic family who kept their private affairs private, often even from each other. Relaying chatty vitriol would only aggravate an open wound. And probably propel Mike further into himself, unsure how to deal with a public outing. We may not have had much, but Mike had his pride. Caring for his family was always Mike's priority, regardless of a perceived ability to do so.

No, tonight we would have spaghetti and, tomorrow, pancakes.

Breaking the thin noodles in half, I dropped them into a pot of boiling water while checking on the simmering sauce-from-a-jar in the pan next to the pasta. I used to make Italian red sauce from scratch, plunging whole ripe tomatoes into bubbling water. Then I'd drain the water and blend the mushy tomatoes with freshly chopped onions, carrots and garlic. Gilly was my sous chef, dicing celery stalks and basil to add to the sauce. We'd pretend we were like Ina Garten, the Barefoot Contessa, whose television show we watched every afternoon on the kitchen television that had hung in front of our island at Oak Lane. We hummed the show's theme song as we scanned through Garten's cookbooks.

"Da da da dum da dum dum dum," we'd sing, just like the opening credits' musical electric keyboard montage. Tasting the garlicky tomato sauce with a spoon, we'd wink in acknowledgment of a job well done.

"How easy is that?" we'd both say in unison, mimicking Garten's famous catch-phrase.

Our dinner that night was no gourmet creation, but we sopped up the store-bought French bread into the store-bought spaghetti sauce and went for seconds. We were hungry for more, starved by the day's events.

At bedtime, I gulped down another migraine pill with a glass of water to erase my dulled throbbing head. Mike lay beside me in the dark.

"How is your head?" he asked.

"It's better," I said, rubbing my forehead.

"Did you ever go to the doctor today?"

"Yes."

"What did he say?"

"He said I'm starting menopause and need to minimize stress, so I've got that going for me," I said with a half-chuckle. It was easier for us to make light of dark things.

"Well, try to get some sleep tonight," Mike patted my arm and turned on his side away from me.

I finally drifted into a deep and medicated sleep. I was floating on a gondola on the Piave River in Venice and drifting along the Grand Canal toward the Palace of the Doges I had once read about in Will Durant's writings of the Italian Renaissance. The doctor's wife and I were seated in the back of the gondola while my doctor stood in the front of the rocking boat, rowing us through the murky waters while serenading us with what sounded like a Vivaldi opera as we drifted past majestic and ornate palaces where the rich and powerful had once lived.

Chapter 7

The Garage: Life in the Tranches

I was knee deep in crap. Standing in our storage unit, I could barely move for all the boxes and garbage bags of stuff piled up.

Our mother-of-all garage sales at Oak Lane depleted much of our belongings, but toward the end of our home departure, the movers—whom we paid for half a day only—were checking their watches. Mike and I started throwing unsold items into empty boxes and when we ran out of boxes, we used garbage bags. My sisters, our unofficial moving coordinators, showed me the fine art of packing improvisation when our storage tools had become few and our emotional reserve had become even less. Cindy labeled bags like a seasoned librarian catalogued books while Julie assessed each room for remaining things that could be bag-worthy.

Now, surrounded by a small mountain of draw-string white plastic sacks that were scented with lavender vanilla "odor block," I apparently had more bag-worthy stuff than I had thought. I made a mental note to never again buy a garbage bag that smelled like a nursing home.

Some friends had graciously offered their Virginia mountain vacation home for us to use during Thanksgiving. It went unsaid, yet not unnoticed, that this would be a difficult holiday for someone like me. I cherished hosting big gatherings with buffet-styled traditions of casseroles, smoked turkey, crock pot ham, homemade pies and sweet tea with enough carb and sugar overload guaranteed to send everyone to nearby comfy furniture for a post-meal nap. My crock pot sold the first thirty minutes into our garage sale and our small apartment had limited seating and cooking capacity. Our dining table and chairs were stored in the garage. I didn't even know where my good china was. Please, God, don't let it be in a bag.

I was in search of the large suitcase I planned to use for the Virginia trip, but damn if I could find it. I got sidetracked opening boxes marked "Family" which had framed photos and scrapbooks. Clearing a spot on the cold concrete floor, I sat down to look at the first scrapbook I ever made for Griffin and was immediately swept back to the anxiety of those early days.

Griffin's birth reminded me that most things in life could not be controlled no matter how hard I tried and how many pregnancy rules I followed. Our son arrived two months prematurely. For six weeks, Griffin was incubated in a teaching hospital's neonatal unit located an hour away from our home. Two weeks into this world, he survived viral spinal meningitis. Even then, Griffin's gentle nature was evident. Other preemies cried throughout the day and night in the Born Too Soon ward while my three-pound little boy quietly nuzzled next to me, tightly grasping my finger with his peanut-sized hand as if to signal not to let go but to help him bust out of that noisy place.

My former preemie was now a five-foot-nine fourteen-year-old who was four months into his freshman year at a private high school that Mike and I were certain we could no longer afford. Not that we ever could afford it. Parenting is often a blend of the irrational and the pragmatic and the heart often dictates over the head. We had always been advocates of the public school system, yet when Griffin got closer to entering high school, we worried if the public high school we were zoned for was too big and impersonal.

His private school had smaller classes with an inclusive sports program where every student had a chance to participate. He instantly connected with his history teacher who spent time after class with him talking about their mutual admiration for military history and the Beatles in equal measure. Griffin was on the golf team. He was thriving. And we were behind on the monthly tuition.

When I tried to find a way we could keep him at the school, I came up short. Even my taking on a few extra freelance stories wouldn't cover the gap. We had other bills that had to be paid. And although Mike and I had more debt than dollars, our combined income just exceeded the maximum amount to qualify for a school financial-needs scholarship. We made too much to keep Griffin in the school and not enough to keep him in the school. Too much and not enough—a monetary quagmire that would follow us wherever we landed. How did we get to this point, I wondered? We had saved and planned and dreamed. But when Merrill Lynch bled, we did, too.

With overly fragrant bags of my earthly possessions around me, I mentally inventoried where Mike and I had gone wrong. Griffin's bike was propped next to the table. Soon, he would get his restricted driver's license. A car for him was not a consideration. A bike would be the only mode of transportation we could swing, but Griffin never asked us for anything. He was the kind of child who appreciated whatever he had, wherever he was. And his parents couldn't keep him in the school he liked. Mike and I decided we'd hold off until after Christmas to figure out a high school move. For now we just wanted to get away to a mountain to escape the valley we were in.

I was good at putting on a brave face that everything would be okay once we got through this rough patch. I said this to anyone who'd ask, myself included. And, lately, I was engaged in a lot of cheery self-talk. Apartment life would be temporary before we'd be back in a home of our own, I'd say with a plastic smile to others. I'd make more money once things turned around for the magazine, which was still recovering from a recession-induced advertising drop-off. Mike would advance at the bank in time. The children were, actually, excited by the notion of living in an apartment that had pool parties for residents every Saturday. Really, we were emotionally stronger as a result, focusing on what mattered most, I'd say, channeling my inner Oprah. What a revelation! We should have done this sooner!

Keeping up appearances was an acquired skill, but if anyone probed more deeply, they'd find my assurances were as empty as the hollow sub-prime mortgages that had brought down the Wall Street big guns and us with it. One of the reasons our country's economy tanked in 2008 was due to a complex and high risk financial maneuver called tranches, a term I had previously never heard of in my Oak Lane life.

Tranche, a French word for "slice" or "portion," is used to describe a security that can be split into smaller pieces and sold to investors. These tranches are chock full of bad sub-prime loans, layers of faux good covering the hollow bad.

As I looked at page after scrapbook page, I realized something. I had become a human tranche. I was hell-bent on portraying an image of a glass-half-full life, and had been, even as a new mother standing in front of my newborn covered with wires and tubes in his intensive care incubator. And I was grinning as if I were standing over a healthy baby at home in his crib even though there was little to smile about at the time the nurse took that picture.

Griffin was losing, not gaining, weight, a troubling sign that would later lead to the meningitis diagnosis. I commuted two hours every day to be with my baby, arriving at the hospital by seven each morning and leaving at eleven o'clock each night. My body informed me I should be nursing, my breasts engorged with the milk that Griffin was too little and too sick to consume. Mike and I were exhausted, snipping at each other on the nightly drive home as the interstate took us further away from our son.

One night, on the way home, we had a meltdown in the McDonald's drive thru. We'd just met with the neonatologist who gave us a crash course in the difference between viral and bacterial meningitis. Griffin's test results were not yet back. We didn't know which kind of illness we were facing although I was praying hard for viral, a macabre plea no parent wants to make. I had cried from the NICU elevator to the hospital garage to the car. While waiting in line to place our order for a cheap midnight dinner of a two-cheeseburger meal deal, I asked Mike if Griffin's hospitalization was covered by our insurance since he was born before we had a chance to update our health benefits. Mike just stared ahead, gripping the wheel.

"Did you hear me?" I asked.

Sometimes, when I brought up a touchy subject matter, Mike would go silent and that spurred me to act like a six-year-old and push even harder.

"What happens if Griffin isn't covered? How much will that cost us? Are you listening?"

Mike turned away from me and stared at the brightly lit menu board next to his car window. Dark circles cupped his eyes. I knew he was at his breaking point, but, hell, so was I, a new mom without her child who was, literally, leaking from every orifice and still aching from the emergency delivery and my glandular overproduction.

"Hey! You can give me the dignity of answering," I said, nudging his arm.

Mike snapped his head toward me.

"Stop it! Just stop it!" Mike said, his voice cracking. "Yes, I think Griffin is covered and I will check tomorrow. Damn it, Amy. I just want..."

Mike took a long, deep breath to inhale back the pain he couldn't suppress, and then he let out quite sobs of helplessness.

"I just want our little man to be okay," Mike cried.

Shaking my head, I started to cry too. There we sat, two scared new parents who couldn't move forward.

A scratchy voice, like Darth Vader's little sister, yelled through the drive-through speaker demanding our order. She had asked for it a few minutes earlier, but her sobbing customers didn't hear.

"Please give me your order," she barked.

Mike started to speak, but he couldn't stop crying. Always the composed one, he could not keep it together anymore.

"Sir, are you okay?" Darth's little sis asked, more annoyed than concerned.

"Yes, just give me two...ahhh... cheeseburgers and...ehhhh....a diet coke," Mike sputtered, but the poor guy was crying so hard, even I couldn't tell what he was saying.

"You want the fish sandwich and two regular cokes?"

"No," Mike cried, but couldn't explain. I was little help, sobbing too as I leaned my head on the passenger door.

This futile exchange went on for a few more minutes before we looked at each other with a "screw it" acknowledgement. We peeled out of the drive-through, hungry and thirsty. An hour earlier I had been standing over my sick son's incubator and had smiled for the camera like a good soldier.

I closed the fabric album in my lap and returned it to the cardboard box thinking how good I had been at convincing myself our current situation was going to be an easy fix. I was neck-deep in morose self-pity when my cell phone rang.

"Hey, honey!"

"Hi, Mama," I said. "Do you mind if I call you back later? I'm trying to find something in our storage unit."

"I saw you on TV!" Mom said excitedly.

"What?" I asked, holding my cell phone in the crook of my neck as I sorted through more boxes and bags.

"Well, it wasn't you, but she looks just like you," Mom said. "She's the woman on one of those home shopping channels who I ordered Thanksgiving candied apples from."

Normally a statement like that would cause one to pause, but that would only be if you didn't know my mother. For Nel Yeary, ordering candied apples for a holiday other than Halloween made complete sense. She embraced the celebratory abnormal. This was the same woman who had a stuffed-animal Valentines bunny wearing a shirt that read, "Some Bunny Loves You." Mike was still learning to adjust to the fact his mother-in-law owned musical-Easter-egg salt and pepper shakers that played Irving Berlin's "The Easter Parade." The pepper shaker always got stuck on the first verse, though a firm wrist shake could easily remedy the problem.

However, I had a twinge of fear that my mother was perhaps not as sound of mind as she had once been. Had I missed the signs of dementia my sisters insisted they saw? Mom forgetting names of family members. Mom losing her sense of direction. Mom asking when Dad was coming home from the hospital.

"I bet she looks better than I do right now," I said brushing off sweat from my brow.

"She was so nice. I was on TV! Well, I wasn't on TV, but my voice was."

"Remember we won't be here for Thanksgiving so I'll have to take a rain check on those apples."

"That's why I ordered extra," Mom boasted.

Great. Something to look forward to when we returned from Virginia, I thought. Turkey-themed caramel coated apples.

"I hope they didn't cost too much," I said, knowing mom would spend her last penny on party favors if she could. When Dad was alive, he'd keep her reined in on her discretionary spending while secretly loving that his wife had a front-door welcome mat with interchangeable holiday figures of Santa, the Easter Bunny and Sam, the Shamrock Lovin' Leprechaun.

"No, they were on sale if I added a case of Christmas candied apples that look like tree ornaments," Mom replied with the enthusiasm of Home Shopping Network Star Joy Mangano.

My phone clicked. The office was calling. I told mom I'd call her back in a few minutes.

I should have let it go to voice mail. The magazine's photographer, whom I'd known for years, was cracking under the pressure of too little pay, too many photo shoots and too much artistic ego. He went off and began railing at me for a perceived injustice he felt I had inflicted on his creative rights. For dramatic emphasis he had put me on speaker phone in the graphic arts department—an outdoor shed next to the Victorian home office—so everyone could hear. Such was the life of the glamorous magazine editor whose job my friends said they envied. A mountain escape couldn't come soon enough.

The next few weeks were a blur of activities with our quick trip to Virginia followed by the move out of The Wellington into our permanent second-floor apartment above our storage unit. Wanting the children to feel at home, I let them pick out paint colors from the apartment's approved selection list. Gilly chose a bright lime green for her bedroom walls and Griffin, a warm khaki tan. We sold Gilly's queen-sized bed, too big for her room, and found a white trundle bed that "popped," as interior designers would say, in front of her key-lime walls. I painted Griffin's twin beds—once Mike's childhood beds—a glossy black. We hung his acoustic and electric guitars on the wall by his window overlooking the apartment pond that was, actually, a large water retention area.

Our new neighbors, whose daughter was a friend of Griffin's, welcomed us with a Christmas pizza party. We returned the hospitality with Chinese take-out the week of New Year's. Cracking open my fortune cookie, I pulled a small paper slip with lottery numbers on one side and a message on the next. "Progress will be in your future" it read.

"Here's to progress for us all!" I said and held up my glass of eight-dollar champagne toward our guests.

"To progress!" cheered our neighbors and Mike.

"To progress!" the kids chimed in, sipping their sparkling apple juice.

Normally, I put about as much stock into a fortune cookie's empty promise as I heeded the advice of an evangelistic talk-show host, but for some reason I kept this fortune of hope and taped it on the refrigerator after putting up the leftover Chinese.

Griffin experienced a change in his immediate future. The inevitable arrived as we transferred him to public high school the first week in January. He took the news with a grace and acceptance that both relieved and killed me. He didn't make the exclusive golf team because it only had a varsity roster, but he made the cross country team and signed up for the high school's ROTC program and jumped into both with optimistic gusto.

Gilly's club volleyball season was gearing up and that meant another hit to our bank account. As volunteer club board members, Mike and I volunteered as much as we could to earn a discount on the club fees. Gilly offered to help, noting she didn't need a new pair of court shoes and knee pads even though hers were visibly worn. I took on a few extra writing projects to lessen the financial stress. My current salary was half of what I had made with the previous magazine, which had given me *The Style Book* gig, and that pay was less than what I had previously made.

One of the perks, however, of being in the faux journalism world, was covering events I'd normally not be privy to. At the end of January each year, Atlanta's AmericasMart, the mecca of all shopping markets for retailers, hosted its annual Home Market Show. The market held prime real estate in downtown Atlanta with skyscraper buildings full of floors of furniture, rugs, pillows, accessories, fake plants and anything else that qualified as home décor. Celebrities would visit to hawk their latest products. Paula Deen and Sandra Lee had their own luxury rug lines. Actress Jane Seymour pushed her home accessories products.

Still clinging to my home and garden passion, I used the market as a reason to cover it for the magazine. As a treat, I took Mike and the kids with me since my normally stingy publisher was paying for our trip, her mea culpa for an increasingly volatile work environment. The market fell on a three-day holiday so the family could play tourists while I salivated over pompom fringed curtains. You can take the girl out of her dream home, but not her love for chintz drapes.

On the second night in Atlanta, I collapsed on my hotel bed as Mike and the kids started watching *Mr. Magorium's Wonder Emporium* on television. Covering market was hard work. I probably had walked five miles between three buildings that each had fifteen floors of stuff-and-more-stuff to write about. Still dressed with my walking shoes on my feet that dangled off the bed, I dozed off, tired but content. Nothing fulfilled me more than being with my family in a hotel. Mike would joke he could take me to a motel in a one-light town and I'd be happy if I were with him and the kids. It was true. I loved the cocooned intimacy of piling together in bed under layers of blankets, watching movies in a well air-conditioned room with blackout shades to block us from the world for a little while.

I heard my phone ring but was too tired to answer. Let it go to voice mail. It rang again. It's your sister Cindy, Mike said, handing me the phone.

Mom's had a stroke, she said. Could be from mixing her medications. We really don't know, she said. She's in the hospital. It's not good. Cindy's voice trailed off.

We drove seven hours to return home early the next day. Mom stayed in the hospital until she was strong enough to go to rehab. She contracted a nasty, highly contagious bacterium that sent her back to the hospital into an isolation unit that required visitors to don masks and protective gowns. Mom was so weak, she couldn't get out of bed.

After a month of see-sawing between hospital and rehab, my sisters and I realized mom could not return to her haven of Valentines bunnies and customized holiday welcome mats. If she got better, she would need constant care. We sold her home and put a deposit on a room at an assisted living facility while mom recuperated at a nursing home.

Before the new owners had moved in, Cindy, Julie and I cleaned up mom's home, choosing what few pieces to keep for our families and selling the rest. Mom wasn't a hoarder, but she had hoarder-ish tendencies, buying and keeping stuff she didn't need. Most of her things were stashed away, and her living areas, where family and guests would visit, remained tastefully decorated with just the right mix of holiday adornment. She, too, was well versed at putting on a good show. I was my mother's daughter. We saved her guest room for last because we knew it was the messiest. Mom used it as a repository for anything she couldn't bear to get rid of.

As we walked down the hall toward it, a pungent sweet-sour smell propelled us to hold our noses as we opened the door.

"What is that smell?" Julie asked, her hand covering her mouth.

"Oh, my gosh," Cindy said and stepped back.

Slowly, I walked toward the acrid stench, opening the closet where Styrofoam coolers marked with "Refrigerate Immediately" labels were stacked on top of each other. Lifting a lid, I discovered the culprit—mom's Thanksgiving candied apples shipped three months prior from the shopping network. This confirmed it—Mom was indeed suffering from dementia. The signs were as clear as the label on the coolers.

Later that day, I visited her. It was time to tell her we had sold her home. My sisters and I had waited until we believed she was up for the news. I did not tell Mom about the apples.

"Mama, you sure gave us a scare," I said as I walked into her room.

"I gave myself a scare, too," she said with a weak laugh.

"I know Julie and Cindy have talked to you about finding a place where you would be around others."

"Honey, I don't want to move," Mom interrupted, her voice breaking.

"I understand," I said. "But we'd all feel better if you had people around you who could take care of you so you wouldn't have to."

Mama stared beyond me like she was looking at someone over my shoulder.

"Your daddy wouldn't want this," she said, starting to cry.

"I'd like to think he'd want us to get the best care for you," I said, so wanting to believe the script I had practiced on the drive over.

"Can't I just go home?" Mom asked, looking at me more as a child than as a parent. Than as a mother who raised four daughters. Than as a businesswoman who had run her own successful company with just a high school diploma. Than as a mom who chaperoned high school dances and made midnight breakfasts afterward at our house. Than as a cherished wife, mother and grandmother who made the holidays special with traditions and decorations in a way only she could create.

Sitting on the edge of her bed, I informed my mother that she was never going home. As I held her hand of bone and skin, we wept together in a room that smelled of lavender and vanilla.

PART THREE: THE APARTMENT, PART DEUX

Chapter 8

Home Office: The Duck Whisperer

In the midst of mom's hospital to rehab to nursing home shuffle, I made a mental note that, when I am older, I will be two shy of enough children to handle caring for me. Julie, Cindy and Donna, my oldest sister who lived out of town, tag teamed with me to care for mom. In between work and family commitments, one of them finished cleaning out mom's house. Another took a shift to be with mom. One called the doctor to understand, once more, in normal human non-doctor language, mom's latest prognosis. Not only had she suffered a stroke, she was also in early-stage dementia. Another sister sorted through mounds of insurance and legal paperwork.

I did meet one new mom in my complex who had more than enough children, fifteen to be exact. This single mom captivated the rapt attention of my neighbors and me. Most mornings when I walked outside to get my newspaper, a neighbor would wave and yell, "Have you seen Mama lately?"

Mama was a duck. Her kids were her baby ducks—or, as my educated children corrected me, ducklings—and they were too cute for words. So cute, in fact, they consumed precious moments in my day when I should have been doing something, anything, but watching Mama and her ducklings. It wasn't my fault that I lived next to a pond of the world's most adorable ducks. In *The Prince of Tides,* author Pat Conroy wrote that geography was his wound. Well, geography became my distraction.

There was nothing particularly extraordinary about the ducks' daily routine, but there was something seductively compelling about them. Maybe it was the way Mama kept a tight rein on all of her babies, paddling at a quick pace in front to form a duck flotilla across the pond, yet always looking behind to make sure everyone was accounted for. Or it could have been her fierce protection of her brood when a menacing bird circled around. She instinctively headed for the shore to nestle beneath a thicket of branches.

Sally, my downstairs apartment neighbor, was part of the Duck Fan Club. Estranged from her husband, Sally was a fellow temporary apartment dweller, closed off from her past and unsure, but hopeful, about her future. When we first moved into our apartment, Sally lived in the building across from ours where she'd sit on a fold-out camping chair each afternoon on the narrow steps in front of her door, greeting neighbors who passed by. She was on the wait list for the apartment beneath us, one with a roomy front porch facing the pond.

"I'll have enough room for real outdoor furniture," she'd tell me more than once with a child-like grin, "perfect for duck watching."

We two became the social commentators of our corner of apartment life. Dan, a handsome divorcee banker, lived nearby, and Sally and I enjoyed speculating about how long his girlfriend of the moment would last. Life paused briefly for all of us when Mama and her crew would waddle up onshore and we'd mill around gaping at them like visitors in front of a hospital nursery.

Sally lived a stone's throw from the pond and the ducks became her friends. It helped that Sally gave them bread crumbs, but they'd stay after their carb appetizer, attentively perched and facing her. The duck family kept their distance from most of us, even when we had bread to share, too, but they were regular visitors outside Sally's place. And she welcomed them with hospitality and conversation. She was our very own duck whisperer.

"How are you doing today?" Sally would coo to her feathered friends. "Your babies are getting big, Mama."

One day, Griffin and Gilly rushed through the front door yelling that Mama had gone missing. Rushing out to the pond, I found no sign of Mama. Sally was already a step ahead of me, standing on our sidewalk toward the parking lot.

"I hope she didn't get run over," Sally said, "Sometimes she'd head toward my car if I wasn't on the porch."

What a smart duck, I thought, before knocking on Dan's door to join the Mama duck search. The ducklings were all together on the shore. I instructed Grif and Gilly to stay with them.

"This isn't like her. She never leaves her babies," Sally said as Dan the Dating Man threw on a shirt and started looking without hesitation. He knew what the ducks meant to us, especially to Sally.

We took different quadrants of the complex. No luck. Then Dan called out.

"I found her!" he yelled.

Sally and I sprinted to the next building facing the pond. We found Mama a few feet away sitting on a hill. She was close enough she could keep an eye on her brood, but far enough for some peace and quiet. We didn't disturb her, though Sally watched until Mama returned to the ducklings about a half hour later. I think she just needed a little "me time."

I could relate. Time alone had become a rarity. Sitting on a hill looked pretty inviting. In addition to caring for mom and the children, pressure was mounting at the magazine office with overworked and underpaid staff. My only private outlet was my home office in the upstairs loft over our family room and kitchen. It wasn't much, but it was mine, sort of.

Far different than my beloved library at Oak Lane Cottage, I used particle board shoe stands as make-shift bookshelves, leaving most of my books packed in boxes in the storage unit. Mike and I shared the loft's laminate counter for computer space and had placed our laptops next to each other. We kept important documents filed in plastic totes beneath the counter that I'd bump with my feet when I was typing.

Attempting to personalize the space, I hung our framed Christmas cards on the loft's wall. I moved my favorite lamp from downstairs to the upstairs' countertop for ambient light. Mike graciously hauled up two flights of stairs mom's bright orange velvet chair, where I'd sit and read after pulling a book off the shoe shelf next to my ankles. Despite my best efforts, my home office was cramped. And it was hot as Hades in the summer.

I returned to my magazine office attic where it was also too crowded and hot. Tempers there were elevated, too. Desperate economic times called for desperate editorial compromise forced by the publisher and the sales department who required us to write more advertorials—paid ads to look like magazine features—the bane of all journalists. Almost everyone was looking for a different job and I reached the painful conclusion that I needed to do so also.

After our resident duck whisperer had moved in beneath us, Mike and I became more proficient in the fragile art of spousal communication, though not by choice, but necessity. Maintaining my writing career wasn't sustainable. I resented the hell out of it and understood why at the same time. Prose doesn't pay the dentist or the groceries or the credit card collection agency. But our small apartment made a discreet conversation impossible, so we went outside. Often. By the pond. By the ducks. Not within earshot of Sally however.

I wanted Mike to save my dreams and he wanted to save us from financial ruin. When we needed to talk about the latest development with my job search or how we'd find a way to stay ahead of our bills, one of us would simply point toward the window, our signal to continue the conversation outside. Yet, what was so strange is that we still whispered as we stood on the soft grass near the water. No matter where we went, Mike and I were uncomfortable with what we had to say and, increasingly, with each other.

"I applied for two more jobs this week, but the search is open for another month," I said quietly, as if Sally and her neighbors and the neighbors next to them could hear us.

"I could try to activate my real estate license, but there may be a policy by the bank preventing outside work," Mike whispered, like he was sharing a secret.

"Well, you should have never gotten the license to begin with since you didn't do anything with it," I whispered back loudly, a skill I had acquired over the course of our hushed talks that often turned into arguments.

Mike waved his hands to try to wipe away the negativity and the conversation, his usual cue for wanting to head inside. With raised eyebrows, he looked up toward our apartment in case the children were staring out the window.

"Why would they be staring out the window," I whisper-yelled. "You just want to avoid doing the hard work of fixing this," I added, sotto voce.

Sometimes Sally was sitting on her patio chair in her front screened porch when we walked past her in silent disaccord, like a funeral march. I'd give a tepid half-smile and wondered if she suspected her fellow duck watcher was in marital trouble.

A friend called to tell me about a job for a utility company in need of a community relations manager. I didn't know a utility pole from a sign pole so I told her I'd think about it. It's a great company, she said, naming off employees whom I knew and respected. Driving home after work, I thought about my so-called writing career that had digressed into editing ads about plastic surgeons and trial lawyers. I felt a migraine coming on.

When I walked into the apartment, I headed straight for the freezer to get a headache-soothing ice pack. That's when I saw it—my fortune cookie slip taped to the refrigerator—"There will be progress in your future." I applied for the job the next day. Two months later, I was a community relations manager.

The company's name? *Progress* Energy.

I needed all the serendipity I could get. My assigned territory covered six counties and twenty cities. The Sunday before I started my new job, Mike drove the children and me to my office, located in another county, so I could get a feel for the daily commute. With each mile I made a mental mark of all the things I resented. Top of the list was Mike. We arrived to my office one hour and forty miles away from home and I had forty reasons I wanted to leave the man who would allow the mother of his children to take a job that would keep her on the road and away from her family.

Why couldn't Mike have the big job with the nice salary? Why did it have to be me? Why was he finding himself, yet again, trapped in a precarious job in the still unsteady banking world that I advised him against returning to? It was easier to target my husband for my unhappiness than focus on other contributing factors. My marriage had become the blame game where there were no winners. Just really angry whisperers.

"Will you have to drive here every day, Mama?" Gilly asked from the backseat.

"Probably at first, but you'll be busy with volleyball after school then we will be home together," I said, thinking, oh, honey, this is one of twenty cities I'll be driving to.

On the drive back, I fumed in tightlipped apprehension in the passenger seat. We were in no position for me to decline the best offer of my life that just might financially save my family. But would it save my marriage?

My first few days on the job went well. My co-workers were incredibly supportive, the work was fascinating and I was surprisingly adept at it. I had to admit there was a spring in my step knowing my salary, combined with Mike's, was better than it had been in years. I wasn't crazy about the commute, but recognized I just might be driving toward the light at the end of the tunnel, financially speaking.

Mom was right all those years earlier when she had said money has a way of making or breaking a relationship. I could turn off the resentment button for a while knowing we could pay our bills on time. Maybe we could start saving a little too, I thought, while driving across the state. My car time gave me lots to contemplate. Heading from city to city, I began fantasizing about my future.

The running joke between Mike and me was that my fantasies were more pragmatic than romantic, no George Clooney for me. Instead, I dreamed about decorating a home—*our* family's home, wherever it might be—room by room. My heart would skip a beat just imagining what a bull-nosed granite top could do for a kitchen. I'd take countertops over Clooney any day. Suddenly, my commute became my mental escape, one decorated room, one mile, at a time. And with the new job I just might have a few pennies to save to make my dream a reality.

The following Thursday, however, I woke up with another headache and washed down a migraine pill with a glass of water before meeting the company's regional vice president at our Ocala office. She invited me to go to a meeting with her in Gainesville. I was grateful for her invitation, wanting to absorb all the knowledge I could from a woman whom I deeply respected. Mike was picking up the children from school that day and my sisters pitched in carline duty the rest of the week. We knew we couldn't sustain this driving arrangement, but hoped to make my work transition as least disruptive for Griffin and Gilly as possible.

Sitting in a board room with one of our company's key customers and our vice president, my head decided it would be a fine time to explode. Normally, I managed my migraines, but this one felt different. I excused myself to take another triptan. By the time we got in the vice president's car after our meeting, the center of my forehead was pulsating pain. I rubbed it until it was red, like Harry Potter rubbed his scar when Voldemort was close by. On the drive back, I kept thinking, let me get home, let me get home. Maybe Mike could stop by the grocery store after getting the kids and grab a rotisserie chicken, something easy for dinner so I could focus on burying my head beneath the pillows. I texted Mike but he never answered. When we pulled into our office, I tried calling him.

No answer.

I left the office for home early afternoon. The kids would arrive with Mike within an hour. Walking in, I saw Mike sitting on the couch in a dark room with the window blinds closed.

"Where have you been?" I asked. "I tried calling you all day."

His eyes welled up.

"I couldn't answer your call because I had to turn in my phone along with the rest of my things," Mike said so quietly I could barely hear him.

"What are you talking about?" I asked.

Mike hesitated before answering. He then turned to me slowly, as if waiting to respond could hold off the inevitable.

"I lost my job."

"What?" I asked repeatedly, hoping for a different answer each time, but each time, the answer was the same.

Banks were still recovering, two years later, from the recession earthquake that had forced them to re-evaluate their strategies and restructure when needed. Mike got restructured out of a job and the earth shook. And just like that, we found ourselves, once again, in the deep crevice of the unemployed and, once again, uncertain, not even one full week with my new job. We'd had a temporary respite from worry for three whole damn days.

.   .   .   .   .   .

The next few months were a dizzying pace of work, commute, work, commute, care for the children, care for my husband, care for my mother. Go to bed. Wake up. Repeat. I worked hard to make a solid first impression with my job not only because that was how I was wired, but also because everything was riding on my ability to stay employed.

A bright spot was that Mom was getting stronger. She would soon leave the nursing home. Each night, after a long day at work followed by dinner and homework and evening sports practices for the kids, I would drive to mom's future home, an assisted living facility. My sisters did the yeoman's work of downsizing mom's things and entrusted me to use what was left to create a sense of home in mom's one-room space.

I was on mental overload, my mind swirling from thinking of job networking for Mike. We'd shared his resume with no solid bites. And my brain was overheated, trying to comprehend a utility vernacular that had more acronyms than the New York Stock Exchange. Tidying up mom's room, I tried to block out the difference between a megawatt and a kilowatt for just a little while.

One Saturday afternoon I went to mom's new place to add a few finishing touches before she moved in the following weekend. I hung the family photo collage dad had made for her and fluffed her bed's decorative turquoise and coral silk pillows. Mom's late sister was an extraordinary knitter whose cream cable-knit blanket covered the end of mom's bed. Spreading out the throw, I lay down on mom's bed and slept so hard and deeply that I was disoriented when I woke up.

For the next few nights, I returned to mom's place, napping on her bed, shutting out the noise.

Our rent was going up and so were our bills. Mike hadn't found steady employment besides his return to the call center as a sales associate. One evening, after returning home from a heated city council meeting two counties away, I had zero balance in my checkbook and an empty food cabinet as I looked across the apartment's kitchen-living-dining room and saw two hungry children. Mike was working the night shift at the call center. I piled the children into the car and went to mom's assisted living facility to "visit" with her, but, really, I timed it so we arrived for dinner so that Griffin and Gillian could eat a hot meal.

Mom was still frail and confused and, in a different way, I was, too. I felt like LeeAndianez Rodriguez, the young girl in western New York who ran a half-marathon after mistakenly thinking she had signed up for a 5K race. She stumbled through the finish line, hours after the other runners, her mother frantic about where she had been. When asked why she stayed the course, she said it wasn't the race she had planned on or trained for, but it was the race she was in.

· · · · · ·

Summer turned to winter. The staff at mom's home was hosting a holiday ball. It was the end of a very long day. I had just returned from an overnight work trip and wanted nothing more than a quiet night in the apartment. But Mom called my cell twice earlier that day asking which holiday sweater I was wearing to her party. I had to go. I wore her favorite Christmas sweater with a cotton-bearded Santa Claus. When Mike, the kids and I arrived, mom was waiting in the lobby with her new friends. She looked beautiful, healthy. Alive.

Music filtered through the dining hall. We started to dance, laughing at our bad moves to "Devil in a Blue Dress." Griffin was pulled onto the dance floor by a sweet woman resident. Mom laughed as her hall mate twirled her around. For a little while, we forgot our worries and danced beneath the well-lit Christmas tree, bright with hope.

As the seasons changed, the ducklings grew almost as big as Mama. They started to test their boundaries, swimming ahead of her while trying to outrace each other. Sally remained on her porch, feeding her duck friends who had an increased appetite for soft white bread.

I wondered what would become of Mama and her ducks? Of us? Griffin got his restricted drivers license and Gilly joined her brother in the ranks of teenagedom and all that came with it. Both were redefining their familial roles, stretching to figure out who they were, separate from me. I missed the early flotilla years where I was in control of my respective pond, not winded by trying to keep up with two teenagers, a new professional career and another unexpected twist to our financial circumstances. But it was the race I was in.

So I kept paddling, hopeful I would one day reach the shoreline.

Chapter 9

Laundry Room: Tumbled

The recession did a number on millions of families, ours included, but I had a front row seat in the theatre of the tortured for my husband. Juggling jobs, caregiving and debt collectors wasn't a picnic for me, but for Mike our situation had become a glaring indictment of his self-perceived inability to provide for us. While my new job took me out of the apartment and into the world of the financially breathing, Mike's lack of a job imprisoned him within the walls of our second-floor, one-thousand square foot home. And he couldn't find it within himself to escape. Any emotional reserve had already been spent. No more lunch with the guys. Or golf outings, even when the invites were for a free nine holes with a friend's membership. Or, more importantly, networking to find work.

"Hey," I said, dropping my keys on the kitchen counter after coming in from work.

"Hi," Mike said, sitting on the couch, watching sports on TV.

"Did you play in that golf tournament Tom invited you to?" I asked.

"No," he said in a clipped tone.

"Why didn't you go?"

Silence.

"It was a beautiful day," I continued. "It would have been good for you to get outside."

Mike shook his head, his dismissive signal for me to drop my questions. Instead, I felt propelled in the other direction and assumed the interrogating style of a reporter. I went all Nancy Grace on him.

"So, you mean to tell me you just sat in this apartment today?"

"No, I had things to do," Mike curtly responded before turning off the TV.

"And you expect me to believe that?" I asked with my hands on my hips.

Mike walked past me into the hallway toward the laundry room.

"Just drop it, Amy," he said as he brushed by me.

Mike was suffering from the effects of a "mancession," a phenomenon of professional role reversal for husbands and wives as an outcome of our country's economic hard times. More wives were becoming alpha to a growing number of beta husbands, or at least that's what the national pundits said on television while pointing to pie charts.

Even before our lives were turned upside down, Mike was not the kind of husband who defined himself or me by traditionally assigned spousal roles. Still, it was both unsettling and exasperating to see Mike struggle from what appeared to be a serious bruised sense of self. I wanted to be like Cher to Nicolas Cage in the movie *Moonstruck*, slapping Mike on the cheek with a firm "Snap out of it!"

Mike never had an oversized ego, something that initially surprised and impressed me for a guy who seemed to have it all. For starters, he was, flat out, the most handsome man I had ever laid eyes on, with jet black hair so thick, my fingers would get stuck if I attempted to run them through it, something that was definitely on my list to try as a hopeful future girlfriend. A longtime runner, Mike had chiseled muscular legs that made my flabby ones go weak just looking at him when he wore his favorite red Nike shorts. His broad shoulders gave me the sense he could fight off ninjas two at a time if ever called upon to do so. Yet, he was humble, almost unknowing, about how drop-dead hunky he was.

Mike's wit matched his physicality. He was whip smart and funny as hell. I could barely keep a straight face during our first conversation at a newly appointed college committee. I was the college representative and he, the community leader serving on the college's foundation. His funny asides about our development of a performing arts series had me in stitches. We two were the youngest committee members by a few decades, a fact made quite evident by the other members' suggestions for performers.

"Let's just stick with good performers for our first season, like the Benny Goodman band," said Howard, the elderly representative from the college's senior citizen institute.

"Don't tell him, but I'm pretty sure Benny Goodman is dead," Mike whispered in my ear. "And I don't how we'll break it to him about Frank Sinatra."

I bit my lip to stifle laughing, but thinking, please, God, let that man whisper in my ear again.

Even better, he visited and cared for his mother like a dutiful son, according to my sister who lived next door to his mom. Only in a small town like Ocala can you get recon info on a potential suitor because your sister lives next to his mother. And your other sister went to high school with him, quickly pulling out her high school yearbook to show black and white photos of a handsome football player shyly smiling for the camera.

And, as I discovered while reviewing potential musical groups for the yet-to-be launched college performing arts program, Mike was an astute and prolific fan of all kinds of music from jazz to big band to classical to iconic (he knew every Beatles song by heart). He was well read and well versed. And he was kind, my goodness, was he kind. The Mother Teresa kind of kind, which I normally veered away from—no one is that altruistic, especially a few of my past boyfriends. But, Mike's gentle spirit guided him to genuinely look for the best in others and when they couldn't be their best, he discreetly helped them out, a gesture I would only find out about from others. I was instantly smitten. Mike was the whole package.

But, now, my whole package was confined to the couch except when he took and picked up the kids to and from school and went to the grocery store. Man, did he love going to the grocery store. Sometimes Mike would go twice a day, picking up the essentials, but either forgetting or choosing to return for "just a few more things," he'd say, when I'd come home at night and see another plastic grocery bag on our kitchen counter. Therapy wasn't Mike's outlet or luxury, but walking down an aisle of fresh fruit and vegetables seemed to recalibrate his mental state.

Which was fine for a little while, but then it wasn't. A visit to our accountant in February altered my patience with our one-job/one-paycheck household. We normally did our own taxes, but needed help assessing the impact of our erratic salaries. Apparently our inconsistent pay had caught the attention of the Internal Revenue Service. When I was working for the magazine, I was a self-employed contractor and that, coupled with Mike's reduced withholding from his former bank job, (we needed every dime we could keep at the time), resulted in us owing the IRS six thousand dollars. Turns out you can be broke and still owe the IRS.

Mike called me on the phone to deliver the bad news as I was driving to an out-of-town work meeting.

"How the hell can we owe money?" I asked, thinking this must be a mistake.

"Your self-employment status resulted in us underfunding our tax contribution," Mike said. "And I probably should have withheld more from my paycheck from the bank at the time."

"I don't get it. We're already in a higher tax bracket than most millionaires pay—I looked it up online the other night," I said, my eyes stinging with tears while trying to concentrate on keeping my car on the road. "We didn't even make that much last year."

"I know. If we could ever get on solid footing, we'd be able to better estimate our withholding," Mike said, weakly adding a punch to my emotional gut. "And because we aren't homeowners, we don't have a mortgage interest that allows us to itemize deductions."

"There's no way we can pay this, Mike," I said as I pulled over into a gas station parking lot. I was crying so hard that I couldn't see in front of me.

"We can ask to set up monthly payments," Mike said. "It won't be easy, but we will have to figure out a way to do this."

Now parked in front of the gas station and its front window displaying a bright orange neon sign advertising hot dogs and coffee as a breakfast combo for $1.99, I slammed my hand on the steering wheel, accidentally hitting the horn. The cashier peered suspiciously at me through the store window.

"No!" I yelled, crying in the driver's seat. "No, it won't be easy and I don't know how we will figure out a way because I am done with coming up with ways to figure things out."

Mike didn't respond. What else could he say? Not much in between the accusations and the verbal javelins I hurled at Mike, who, I said, worked harder at making a trip to the grocery store than to a job counseling appointment at the state's workforce agency.

And he let me. He could've offered his own biting evaluation of how my job choices contributed to this mess, how my writing career was poorly timed, but he didn't. So I threw everything at him I could think of. But, I refrained from hitting the car horn again. The cashier walked toward the store entrance with a concerned look to see if he should help the hysterical woman in her car or ignore her and check on those greasy hot dogs on the rotating grill by the slushie machine.

Mike finally replied, repeating we would figure it out. If he said it enough, maybe it would be true. From my vantage point then at a gas station in the middle of nowheresville, the only thing I could figure out was how to get it together, wipe off my smudged mascara, blow my nose, buy a cold bottle of water from the skittish cashier and head to my meeting.

"Are you okay to drive?" Mike asked quietly. "Any way you can just come home?"

Holding the cell phone, I stared ahead as tears dripped onto my khaki suit jacket and left wet dark drops on the lapel.

I wasn't okay to drive, but I would take a few minutes to compose myself. I was a few minutes late for my scheduled appointment, but reached my destination and walked into the conference room with the false confidence of a runway model. I shook hands and exchanged pleasantries while attributing my puffy eyes to allergies. Pollen is so bad this time of year, I said, feigning a smile. Let's get started, I added, and pulled out documents from my binder. For the rest of the meeting, I nodded and contributed only when necessary, thinking of nothing else but one thing.

Six thousand dollars.

.   .   .   .   .   .

Mike elevated his job search while adding a few more hours of work at the call center. Nothing like insurmountable debt to kick things into high gear. Household responsibilities added to Mike's pressure as my job became more complex with an unprecedented company issue in one of my communities keeping me busy and away from home. Mike took care of the kids, made their breakfast, packed their lunches and had my dinner covered in foil on a plate waiting for me when I got home at night, which, most of the time, was after Griffin and Gillian had already eaten in between homework and volleyball and track practice.

Mike and I were parental ships passing in the night, or, in our case, the apartment parking lot. As I arrived home, Mike was heading off to work his night shift. If we were honest with each other, our minimal interaction was welcome. No good would have come from a prolonged exchange, that much I knew. When we tried to talk—at our usual spot outside near the pond and by the ducks—the conversation quickly digressed into an accusatory argument laced with resentment, frustration and fear. Better to stay inside. And I did.

On weekends I wrote marketing plans for some friends' businesses to bring in a few extra dollars. I pared down an already pared-down discretionary budget. I clipped more coupons. And I scanned job sites for Mike. We had four weeks before we began paying the first of umpteen-some months to pay off our IRS debt. I had no idea how we'd manage it. I went to work every day and focused on the things I could influence and ignored the things I couldn't, sort of like the serenity prayer except for the wisdom and courage.

Mike was in charge of laundry duty, too. The children pitched in, discovering the importance of separating whites from colors and the magical powers of static-free dryer sheets. Our laundry room, the size of a coat closet, was across the hall from the children's bedrooms. It also housed the water heater, making for tight quarters if more than one person tried to clean a load of clothes.

When time allowed, however, I tried to help. It made me feel useful, but it was also strangely satisfying. Standing over a warm pile of towels fresh from the dryer was comforting despite the fact my butt hit the water heater when I bent down. The simple routine of folding clothes—touching Griffin's favorite Star Wars T-shirt, flattening out the wrinkles in Gilly's cotton dress—grounded me. Sometimes, on the rare occasion I was alone in the apartment, I'd turn the dryer on for thirty minutes, lay on Gilly's daybed across the hall, and fall into a dreamy-but-not-sleepy state, soothed by the dryer's rotating tumbler turning its contents with the clink-clink-clink of metal buttons from Griffin's jeans hitting the ceramic barrel.

I missed my laundry room at Oak Lane which had also been my craft/wrapping/mama's TV room. Right off the garage, the long narrow room connected to the family room and had a large window to the back yard, perfect for watching the kids play while I did laundry. I painted the walls a bright, sunny yellow and placed a small television on top of corrugated shelving above the washer and dryer and I watched home and garden shows while folding a warm set of sheets. A long counter with cabinets above and below framed the back of the room, an ideal spot for my craft supplies. I dedicated a corner of the room as a "painting nook" with watercolors and canvas. I wasn't much of a painter, but I enjoyed the meditative process that came with it. When one of my best friends turned forty, I invited her over for "Wine and Wishes" and we painted our dreams and goals on stretched canvas panels. The chardonnay was a huge creative boost. I improvised.

In this space I also did a ton of gift wrapping, inspired by my mom. She always had a gift closet with tubes of wrapping paper, bags, tissues and trinkets in case we needed to give a last minute present. Next to the washer was a bookcase, substituting as my gift closet, where I placed storage bins of bookmarkers, candles and gift boxes. I stored extra food in the room, too, using a spare refrigerator for frozen casseroles, meat and sodas. It was the ultimate multi-purpose room.

And, as much as I missed my sunny and crafty respite, I longed even more for the domesticity that had gone with it. Housework may have been considered a feminist's final frontier, but for me it was a reminder of a role I no longer held. It wasn't that I relished washing dishes or cleaning toilets, rather it was that I wasn't given the choice to stay home. Or that's how I saw it. I couldn't let go of who I had to be in my marriage. And the kicker of it all was that Mike accepted his shift in responsibilities—the increased child care, the chores, the running of the endless errands—better than I accepted my part of the deal. Forget the mancession, I struggled with a momcession and suffered from the heartburn of not caring for my children the way I had for the first twelve years of their lives.

.   .   .   .   .   .

In the world of utilities, springtime meant storm time in Florida. To be prepared, my company held a weeklong storm drill with intensive training that made my head spin like a vertical swirl in the eye of a hurricane. Our regional storm team began each drill day with six a.m. storm calls and concluded around eight p.m. with daily lessons learned. I skipped lunch one day so I could study my storm notebook. By the last storm call, I was ready for a lazy night at the apartment. And carbs, lots of carbs, my go-to stress reducer.

I arrived home late, craving my family and food. But neither was there. The place was empty and messy, piles of notebook paper spread across the kitchen table. And the kitchen was devoid of any evidence that someone, say my husband, had been cooking. As I walked up into the loft to drop off my work tote, I heard the door open.

"Hey," I yelled.

"Mama!" Gilly and Griffin said in unison and ran up the stairs to give me a hug before heading back downstairs, noting dad said they had to take a bath before dinner.

"*Before* dinner?" I asked Mike as I walked downstairs to the kitchen.

"Did you get my voice mail?" Mike asked as he opened a bag from an office supply store.

"Nooooooo, I did not. I've been on category four hurricane storm calls all day," I said. "What's for dinner and why so late?"

"It's been a crazy day. I left you a message to see if you'd mind picking up a pizza on your way home," Mike said before taking a deep breath.

"I didn't play my messages. I just wanted to get home," I said shaking my head. "So, I guess this means we don't have dinner." Before Mike could respond, I felt the need to continue.

"I just have to ask, what did you do all day that kept you from making dinner? The kids were in school and you were home," I asked/said/declared.

I wasn't up for a fight, but I was hungry and angry, and hangry don't tolerate much.

"Well, Gilly forgot her lunch and called me the minute I got home so I turned around and dropped off lunch to her school, then Griffin called and said the deadline for the field trip fee was moved up to today and he couldn't go if he didn't bring a check so I ran to his school and saw Mrs. Johnson who asked if I could stay in her class for her reading session because the other volunteer parent called in sick last minute and that lasted until after lunch when I went to the store to buy poster board for Griffin's science project, then I picked up Gilly from school then Griffin then back here so Gilly could change for volleyball practice and it was my day to pick up Abby and take her and Gilly to the gym, that's when Griffin called and his ride to track practice didn't show so I rushed back to the apartment to take him to the high school, I thought I could grab dinner after but he said he needed one more thing for his science project so I ran back to the store, picked up Gilly then picked up Griffin and now I'm here," Mike said exasperated. "So, no, I didn't have time to make dinner. I'm sorry to have inconvenienced you with my call. I know what kind of week you are having and I thought it would be easiest to just get a pizza, but apparently, I was wrong."

For a minute, we stood in silence. I gave Mike a chance to catch his breath. His heavily lidded eyes were cornered with crow's feet and I noticed a small patch of gray in that thick Mangan mane framing his temples which I didn't recall being there. Mike's once strong shoulders slumped dejectedly toward his chest that was now emptied from the release of all that he had kept inside.

That's when a miracle occurred, not a big one, more a brief brightness, like what Florida's summer lightning bugs gave off while flying near our pond. Serenity washed over me, the effect of spilling out every last drop of fight in me, allowing me a release, too.

Looking at my weary husband, I realized something had happened between us. We were both reacting to a dynamic different than what we first had in our marriage. We were now treading paths the other once followed. It wasn't Freaky Friday-ish, but close. And no matter how hard we tried, we couldn't trade roles and go back to the familiar.

I gently touched his shoulder, more like a reassuring friend than his wife of twenty-one years. No, you weren't wrong, you're just tired, I said. I know this life, I'd lived it, I told him. It's not a big deal. I'll call and order the pizza. I'll help with Griffin's science project, too, I said, clearing the papers on the table to make room for some high-carb pepperoni pizza. For many years, I didn't think Mike appreciated all the family minutia that I had to deal with on top of working full-time. Now he was living it, at least the family minutia part. I think he got the picture. I did, too.

That night we had to decide what to do about the apartment's rent increase notice, something neither one of us had found time to discuss.

"We could rent a house for what we were paying here," I said to Mike who mumbled something, a probably-but-I-don't-have-it-in-me-to-look sigh as he closed his eyes.

Clicking through rentals online, I found a cute home in our old neighborhood. It was actually for sale, but I knew the owner, who didn't live there, but bought and renovated older homes. Maybe he'd consider a lease-option for a year or two. The housing market was still recovering and a renter was better than a vacancy. This would give us a place that felt more like home, I hoped. Maybe more like somewhere we remembered in what seemed like another life.

I fell asleep that night with my laptop screen still glowing on my lap.

PART FOUR: HOUSE OF GRAY

Chapter 10

The Driveway: Ghost Visitor

Gilly's voice was frantic and urgent—an unfamiliar tone for my usually calm and happy fourteen-year-old—when she called me on my cell phone. I had just pulled into our driveway after work. Another mom was dropping her off after high school volleyball practice.

"Mama, I can't remember our address. We've been driving around and I don't know which street to turn on," Gilly said, her voice breaking. We had just moved into the new house rental and were all a bit disoriented. Even I found myself driving to the apartment, only to turn around once I had pulled into the parking lot.

"That's okay, sweetie," I said. "Tell Miss Beth to turn right on Fourteenth Avenue off Eighth Street when she reaches the four-way stop sign."

Gilly let out a big sigh.

"How'd practice go?" I asked, a veiled parental attempt to change the subject.

"It was fine," she said quietly. "I just want to get home."

Hanging up the phone, I turned off the car's ignition and sat in the driver's seat for a few minutes, surveying the view in front of me as the sun began to slowly fall from the sky behind towering pine trees with brown-needled limbs hovering over our house like daunting strangers. The circular driveway curved in front of the house. Only once before did I live in a place with a circular drive, and I swore I'd find another. That kind of entrance was more inviting than a side driveway near a garage that you'd have to keep closed to hide all the junk inside as guests walked by to reach the front door.

As nice as the concept of the driveway was, it lacked in practicality. Our landlord must have run out of money before finishing it and opted for a cheap gravel top. At first I was thrilled with the gravel paving, a nice homage to the kind of driveway typically found next to a cedar shingle home in the Hamptons, my ultimate dream home. Jack Nicholson and Amanda Peet pulled up to Diane Keaton's Hamptons house on a gravel driveway in *Something's Gotta Give*, my favorite movie mainly because of the house and the coastal property. Soft pebbles crushed beneath the tires on Nicholson's BMW in the film's opening scene. Ahhhhhh. The crunchy sound of money.

Years earlier I had downloaded the movie's house plans, carrying them around in my "Amy's Dream Home" three-ring notebook, but my driveway wasn't paved with expensive small stones imported from the rich world. It was covered in porous gray rocks that caved into deep ruts after a few cars drove over them. When it rained, water filled the troughs, funneling in on them like when Moses closed the Red Sea and drowned the Egyptians. After a thunderstorm, I'd walk out to my soggy rock driveway, hold out my broom with my arms wide open like Charlton Heston in *The Ten Commandments* and exclaim "Behold his mighty hand!" demanding the water to part from the ruts. No such luck.

And when there was no rain, there was dust. Lots and lots of rock dust after cars pulled in, swirling a cloudy sooty dust bowl. As if that weren't enough, I walked into the house with tiny rocks embedded in the bottoms of my shoes making me sound like Savion Glover when I tap-tap-tapped on our entryway's ceramic floor. Something had to give, alright.

Across the street, neighbors I hadn't met were playing with their children in the front yard. Another neighbor who lived next door always waved when she drove by. I'll meet them soon, I'd tell myself. Then the weekend would slip into another work week.

We'd lived in this rental since July. It was now early October and I still didn't know much about my new home, the one painted in a dark slate gray like the inky clouds in a Florida thunderstorm. Leaving the apartment was, initially, a mood-booster for our family. We were back in our old neighborhood a mile away from Oak Lane. The house had a small kidney-shaped swimming pool that quickly became central command for entertaining friends and family on hot summer days. Griffin and Gilly picked new paint colors for their rooms—khaki for him and lavender and navy for her—and enjoyed the split-bedroom plan that gave them more private space than the tiny apartment. kitchen was an open concept design with a gas stovetop set in a gloriously-wide island that connected to the family room with wide sliding glass doors leading to the swimming pool. I dusted off my Ina Garten cookbooks and made shrimp scampi and oven-baked steaks while listening to Chet Baker and Frank Sinatra on my iPod.

And Mike found a job as the head of a foundation for our community's local homeless shelter and food pantry, a good match for a man with a heart to help and a rolodex with former banking clients who wanted to help, too. His salary was half what he made at the bank, but his office was at home, an intangible benefit affording flexibility to help with our high schoolers.

Things were slowly getting better, so why did I walk around with a cloak of unease from a phantom fear that haunted me? I couldn't explain it, but I felt it, standing in the kitchen over a pot of linguini, lounging in the pool with a too-bright sun zeroing in on me and sitting in my car in the pebbly driveway, serving as my daughter's navigation system on a night of the lost. I feared becoming too attached to this house where we were borrowing space and time for a little while. Hell, I couldn't remember our address either.

• • • • • •

While I no longer had my decorative wooden pumpkins or harvest spice candles, Fall remained my favorite season. Nothing like an autumn leaf to lift one's spirits. And both children celebrated birthdays around the same time the sunshine state decided it was time to turn down the thermostat below eighty degrees. On a cool October evening, Griffin and his friends circled around a fire pit by the pool as we sang happy birthday to my first-born. Sixteen years. Grif was a legal driver and in his sophomore year of high school. He took his first round of college entrance exams as preparation for his junior year that would be here before I knew it. College. Yikes. I blinked. As Grif leaned in to blow out the burning candles on his vanilla cake, I made a silent vow to inhale every moment with him. With Gilly, too. To not be so caught up in the challenges of life that Mike and I had faced that I forgot to appreciate what was good and right in my life.

Keeping my promise, I revisited a former Halloween tradition. Boo Bags. When the kids were little, we'd spread out an assembly line of paper, bubble gum, lollipops and dollar toys on Oak Lane's laundry/craft room counter. Then we'd fill small, white, lunch-sized bags with the candy and treats, decorated with black Sharpie-penned ghost faces on the front of the bag. When we were extra crafty, we'd cut out a Casper-ish ghost on poster board and write "You've Been Boo'd!"

Griffin and Gillian invited friends over at dusk, all dressed in *Mission*

Impossible black. We loaded kids, Boo Bags and ghost signs into my mini-van. We had a list of our hits, I mean our friends' homes, whom the kids would stealth-like sneak up to their front door and leave the Boo Bags on the steps, tape the Ghost Sign to their door, and then run like hell back to my idling getaway car, laughing the whole way. A classic ring-and-run.

Griffin took a hall pass on continuing the tradition. Not too many sixteen-year-old boys handed out craft bags tied in orange and black silk bows. He invited a few of his guy friends over to watch the bag assembling festivity and nibble on Sour Patch Kids before the boys retreated to our family room to play video games. But Gilly and her volleyball friends, some of whom were juniors (thrilling Gilly, the freshman, to no end), were ready to rock and ring by placing their ghost bags into a large basket.

Blasting top hits on my car's satellite radio, we mapped out our Boo stops. The first drop-off was a close one. The girls inched up to their friend's house and placed the bag on the doorstep. Just as they taped the Ghost on the door, the front entry light turned on. They froze.

I rolled down the window of my car, parked close by.

"Girls, hurry, come on" I yelled/laughed like a comedic drill seargent. "Move! Move! Move!"

Gilly, now hunched by the front window bushes, glanced at me, then busted out laughing. Her Boo comrades were stuck at the front as a woman's shadow appeared closer to the glass door. Now, this is what I loved about my daughter. No matter the situation, real dire or fake dire, she'd find a reason to laugh, and in a raucous guffaw belying her petite frame.

"Mama, we got this!" Gilly said between fits of hearty cackling. She motioned with her hands to her friends. "Girls, let's move it out!"

They raced across the yard and leapt into my car just before I pulled away, narrowly missing the puzzled mother opening the door. Boo Bag Hit Number one accomplished!

In the car on the way to our next stop as Madonna and Justin Timberlake's "5 Minutes" boomed through my stereo, Gilly, sitting in the front passenger seat, grabbed my arm, her bottom lip raised in a sweet grin.

"I love you, Mama. Thank you for doing this," my blue-eyed ghost-stalker said, squeezing my arm in our secret Morse Code Love Signal. Three squeezes meant, "I. Love. You." Then I squeezed her hand four times. "I. Love. You.

More." followed by the conclusion of one last signal clutch by Gilly, with four staccato-speed love presses from her hand.

"Im-poss-i-ble."

Some days, I believed it was impossible to love her and Griffin any more than I did. Then another day would arrive and my heart would expand a little more. I'd been around enough children to know I hit the lottery with a really extraordinary son and daughter. They were wise beyond their years, appreciating the sweet spot of life when it came their way, like a dreamy rainy evening listening to a radio show with mom and dad, or a family trip where the best part of traveling was playing cards on our soft hotel beds. They asked very little of Mike and me, barely venturing into the bratty adolescence or indignant repulsion often seen in their generation. And, blessing among blessings, they acknowledged our gestures of love in big and small ways.

Pulling into the grassy side yard of another Boo Bag home, I watched Gilly and her friends run up to the door and I thought I was the luckiest mom in the world.

We greeted November with another birthday, Gilly's fifteenth. We honored her with our family tradition of waking up the birthday honoree early before school. Her door was adorned with blue and yellow crepe paper spiraling to the floor. She drowsily walked into the kitchen where we had balloons, presents and a glazed chocolate doughnut with a candle.

"Happy birthday to you, happy birthday to youuuuuuu," Mike, Griffin and I sang as Gilly sleepily walked into the kitchen.

She began to open her presents. Suddenly, Gilly stopped and stared into space, dropping her gift to the floor.

"Gilly?" I asked, laughing, thinking she was joking as if she couldn't believe her good fortune of getting gifts *and* a balloon *and* a doughnut with a candle in it.

Staring zombie-like, Gilly started to shake her hands in a rotational jerk like she was rubbing a steering wheel. It was subtle and quick.

"Okay, very funny," Mike said smiling, "We know you always wanted a chocolate glazed donut so Mama and I saved up for it."

But, Gilly didn't respond. Griffin tapped her shoulder.

"Gil, you ok?" he asked.

Gilly shook her head like she was coming out of a trance, then rubbed her eyes and picked up the birthday card Griffin had made for her and started to read.

She laughed at his card with a sibling humor only those two understood. Mike picked up her present from the floor.

"You're a silly Gilly," Mike said and handed Gilly her present before setting the table for breakfast.

As Gilly opened her presents, the foreboding knot in my stomach returned.

"Mama, I love it!" Gilly said holding up her new sweater before tackling me with one of her bear hugs that instantly made my worry vanish. At least for a while.

That night, I went to Gilly's high school gym to pick her up from volleyball practice. Heather, one of her teammates, had a father who was a doctor and close friend. Hunched on wooden bleachers, Heather's dad and I exchanged pleasantries as the girls put away the balls and net. He asked about Gilly and her birthday. I casually mentioned her incident that morning—dropping her gift and staring—not planning to, not really thinking anything of it, but something made me tell him. He squinted his eyes, saying nothing, just nodding.

Later at home, after having a late dinner, I walked into my bedroom to take a bath. My cell phone rang. It was the Heather's dad.

"Hi, Amy, I hope I'm not interrupting dinner," the doctor said.

"No, not at all," I said instantly worried why he had called.

"Look, I don't want to alarm you, but after I saw you tonight, I asked Heather if she had noticed Gilly having staring spells during practice or at school.'

"Uh-huh," I uttered, finding the bed to sit on. My legs were quivering.

"She said she had and, well, look, this is probably nothing to worry about, but I'd like to refer Gilly to a neurologist and order an EEG," he said.

"Oh, really?" I asked trying to process how I went from celebrating my daughter's birthday thirteen hours earlier to now discussing testing her brain.

"We'll do this just to be safe," he said reassuringly.

"Yeah, just to be safe," I repeated, thinking Gilly was just sleepy earlier today, that's all. She dropped a present. Big deal. I drop things all the time. I stare into space sometimes, too, especially when staring out the window while eating a cherry popsicle over the kitchen sink. It happens to everyone.

The next morning, Mike and I sat in a neurologist's office, our metal chairs next to Gilly, who was lying on a patient bed with flat, metal electrodes attached to her scalp. During her EEG, I tried to block out every possible medical cause I'd Googled the night before, but by the end of the day, when we returned home, we received the call that confirmed the diagnosis: absent seizures, a neurological "firing" of the brain off both sides.

Gilly had just turned fifteen and had epilepsy.

Mike and I walked around the next few weeks in a fog, stunned by our daughter's condition, yet only falling apart when she couldn't see. Our bedroom—painted by our landlord in a deep burnt orange like the inside of an overripe apricot—became our crying room, enveloped in sadness and fear. Our minds whirled as we learned about epilepsy. Helplessness and guilt overcame us. Why couldn't we have epilepsy? Not Gilly. Not our sweet daughter who had just begun her freshman year at the International Baccalaureate Honors high school.

Gilly was a hard worker, in school and on the court. She was athletic and academic, balancing both with a healthy social network of friends of all ages. She had a place reserved in her abundant heart for the elderly, picking up a conversation with senior citizens in a restaurant or store as if they were her relatives. She was Gilly Girl, her nickname shared in beloved admiration by all who knew her, even her new high school principal.

"There's our Gilly Girl!" her principal would say when he'd see her after a volleyball game just the second before Gilly would embrace him in one of her signature hold-on-tight bear hugs. Her teammates knew if Gilly Girl was heading their way, get ready, because she'd leap into their arms with her legs and arms wrapped around their bodies as they carried her, papoose-style, across the gym floor.

But, epilepsy, dear God.

High school is mortifying enough, let alone the fear you'll have a seizure without warning, an insidious visitor sucking your soul into catatonic submission before leaving you helpless and physically violated. Once, when I was teaching history at the community college, one of my students had an epileptic seizure during my class. Her head jerked back and hit the desk behind her as she began to convulse, slumping into the classroom aisle. She recovered after a few minutes, but it felt like an hour as she looked around confused, with drool dripping from the corners of her bloodied lip. I remember thinking, what a dreadful condition.

Rationalizing Gilly's diagnosis, we took comfort in what I referred to as the modicum of the macabre. At least Gilly had absent seizures, not a brain tumor. An MRI had ruled that out. And not the more visibly frightening form of epilepsy, a gran mal leaving one to flail and jerk and bite and pee while unconscious, like the one my college student had. Staring spells aren't that bad, right? That's what I told myself over and over. And she could grow out of the spells according to her doctor and the multiple web sites I was instructed not to read, but bookmarked on my laptop every night. But, would she?

"Mama, will I have this forever?" Gilly asked me when we found ourselves alone in her room.

"The doctors say this is treatable and not necessarily permanent," I answered honestly and optimistically.

"One day at school last year, John in my chemistry class had a seizure," Gilly said, her eyes welling with tears. "And I remember thinking I would never want to have to deal with that."

Sitting on her daybed, I rubbed her arm and remembered my college student, a story I chose not to share with Gilly.

"Then we will do everything to get you healthy," I said doing my best to reassure her.

"But, what if I have a gran mal like John?" she asked crying.

"Your medicine will prevent that from happening and will help your brain to heal just like the doctor explained," I said wrapping my arms around her.

"And what about volleyball? The doctor said sleep deprivation is a trigger. How can I go to early morning practices?" Gilly asked, now softly sobbing into my chest.

"You will go about your life doing the things you want to do while also taking care of yourself." I said. "We will all get into a good sleep pattern, too. But, for now, let's just take things one step at a time. Let's not cross..."

"...any bridges we haven't reached," Gilly finished my sentence as she wept, patting me on the back in her tender way as I reminded myself to heed my own words, which I had so often repeated to my children.

Gilly worked hard not to let her condition define her, yet she respected the influence it had in her life. She got eight hours of sleep almost every night. She stayed hydrated. Took her meds exactly as prescribed morning and night. And she focused on her I.B. classes, enjoyed her friends and left any anxiety she had outside the gym. When she ran onto the volleyball court, she was a competitor, digging spiked balls that came her way with an intensity befitting a real fighter.

During this time we were introduced to a new tribe of friends, those who had epilepsy or had friends with epilepsy or knew doctors who specialized in epilepsy.

They circled around us, gave insights on anti-seizure medicine, gave us their cell phone numbers and, graciously, answered our calls again and again. And they connected Gilly to a well-respected and compassionate doctor at the teaching hospital at the University of Florida in Gainesville.

So this was it. The unshakeable shadow, the ghost of an unexplainable misgiving, which followed me everywhere. This is what I had felt in my bones, in my throat, in my stomach, in my heart that I couldn't explain all the months prior. A premonition, my mother would say, something I'd previously dismissed as hooey. Our move to the House of Gray should have been the salve to heal the wounds of our past three years. Talk about hooey. How superficial of me to obsess over a place to live when I should have noticed the warning signs of my daughter's condition. But, were there warning signs?

"What could we have done to have kept this from happening to her?" I cried to Mike one night in our wailing room with the bedroom door closed. He held me in his arms and wept onto my shoulder. There was nothing he could say. We stood by our bed, embraced in a pain that a new home or new job or new whatever could not erase.

"I don't know," Mike wept. "But I know this. We will do anything to help our Gilly get better. Anything."

It was true. We would do anything. I'd sell everything I owned to give Gilly the best medical treatment possible. I'd move anywhere to give her access to the best doctors, although I was grateful it appeared that the very best lived just forty-five minutes away. It was liberating, really, because nothing else mattered except getting Gilly healthy. Nothing. Not an open-concept kitchen or house in a kidney-shaped swimming pool. If leaving everything meant Gilly could have been healed, I would have raced to my car and peeled out of the rocky driveway with the badly landscaped front yard.

Instead, the only thing I could do was to be her constant advocate and protector and ensure she'd get the best care and the right treatment and eliminate everything else that got in the way. And, at the moment, her new medicine was getting in the way, making Gilly lethargic and dizzy. Our options were limited. Only a few anti-seizure medications could treat her kind of epilepsy and this one, the one making her sick, was the best of them all. It could also give her a potentially fatal rash. So, we waited and watched closely.

One afternoon, lying on the couch, Gilly started to cry, not from pity, that wasn't in Gilly's nature, but from exhaustion. On my knees, I leaned on the couch cushion close to her, clutching her arm three times.

I.Love.You.

She looked up, giving me a faint smile as if to reassure me. She squeezed my hand.

I.Love.You.More.

Oh, no, sweet Gilly. No. Fighting back tears, I grabbed her hand.

Im-poss-i-ble.

Simply impossible.

Chapter 11

The TV Room: Goat Rodeo

When Gilly was eight years old, she had decided she would be a mandolin player. It was on the night our family traveled out of town to see Garrison Keillor's *Prairie Home Companion* live show, the night we came to appreciate the spellbinding powers of a mandolin.

Keillor introduced guest performer Peter Oshtroushko on stage to "play a tune for the fine folks" on his mandolin. Oshtroushko nestled the teardrop, string instrument close to his body, and, bowing his head, paused for seconds that felt like minutes as if to say grace for what was about to happen with no regard for the pregnant silence in the packed auditorium. Mercifully, he began to play. Tenderly plucking the chords to create a memorable, melodic sound, the mandolin player whom I'd never heard of before taught me what magic sounded like. He strummed his original composition "Puckett's Farewell," a haunting, homage to the late baseball Hall of Famer Kirby Puckett, but, truly, I felt he was playing for me.

We drove back to our hotel sensing the earth had moved, or at least the northern part of Florida shifted a little. Even at young ages, Griffin and Gilly seemed to recognize we had witnessed something special. Gilly announced she would be a mandolin player who would travel the world one day.

"It was magical!" Gilly shouted with her iconic smile as she jumped up and down on the hotel bed. "I'll have my own band, too."

Gilly, the blue-eyed mandolin player who traveled the world with her All Star Magic Band. I liked it.

The mandolin became my favorite sound, harkening back to that special night. This was around the same time that Griffin picked up the guitar as his instrument of choice. He began playing an acoustic, making his mama's heart swell. Then he became a teenager who strummed The Beatles, Creedence Clearwater Revival and Neil Young, making his dad's heart swell even more. Close enough for me.

"Soon, we will buy you a mandolin," I promised Gilly.

But, first, we bought Oak Lane Cottage, moving in two months after attending the Keillor concert. For the next five years, music filled every room in our house among the oaks. The kids and I danced around the kitchen counter to the latest pop songs, lip syncing every word to the Black Eyed Peas "Let's Get It Started" in a perfect imitation that would make Jimmy Fallon proud. It helped pass the time while our chocolate chip cookies were baking. Mike and I swayed our hips in salsa rhythm to the Buena Vista Social Club while making dinner and, fittingly, mojitos with homemade simple syrup and muddled mint leaves for authenticity. And in keeping with my father's tradition of dancing with me after dinner, Mike, Griffin, Gilly and I usually found an excuse to dance after dinner on the wood floors in the foyer. Big band or jazz was often our choice, but sometimes we'd mix it up and play a contemporary Michael Buble just for kicks.

Every once in a while, though, Gilly would play one of several of her Peter Oshtroushko CDs, reminding me she'd love to learn to play the mandolin. Then we left Oak Lane and, for the most part, the music that went with it.

.　.　.　.　.　.

In December after Gilly's epilepsy diagnosis, I attended a lecture at a business that hosted monthly presentations by nationally recognized speakers on topics of interest to the community. Through my job, I agreed to sponsor one of the presentations. I told the event coordinator to fit me in on a slot that needed funding, not paying particular attention to the lecture I was sponsoring until I arrived that night. As a sponsor, I had a front row seat, reserved for key sponsors. In front of me was a big screen projected with the one topic in the world I had worked intentionally hard to avoid. The speaker was an investment advisor.

The topic? The rise and fall of the stock market with investment strategies for the future.

It was too late to get up and leave, so I sat there, anxiously hoping the next hour could pass quickly and mercifully.

The speaker, dressed in a suit befitting someone who had speculated the market very well, spoke of the year 2008.

"This was a time that we, as a nation, almost lost all of our bearings," he said.

My husband and I lost our jobs, our home.

"You couldn't get any lower, market wise, than what occurred on the Dow Jones in 2008," he continued to an audience nodding their heads in somber acknowledgement.

There I was again, remembering the time I went with Griffin and Gilly to mom's assisted living facility to visit at dinner time so my children could eat a hot meal.

Yes, I knew low.

The speaker said the drastic stock market decline made setting corrections even more worrisome.

"The problem with playing the market is that it's like going to Vegas," he said, eyebrows raised. "You might get it right at first, but then nothing works, creating massive liquidation."

I liquidated practically everything my family owned, even Dad's cherished music collection. I didn't have the room for it in the apartment and who knew big band music sold well at garage sales?

I'd liquidated my magic.

Holding one of his signed books, the prolific economist offered the audience a quiz with one of his books as the prize.

"What stock was the worst performing stock in 2009 but is now the best performing stock?"

The audience was stumped.

Not me.

I knew, but could not stomach to say. It was Bank of America, I wanted to scream, the bank that overleveraged and had bought Merrill Lynch and "corrected" its books to eliminate positions like my husband's so the multi-million dollar merger could be complete. So the Merrill CEO who bought an eighty-seven thousand dollar area rug for his office could seal the deal. So both CEOs could walk away from their botched merger with well over forty-four million dollars each in stock and benefits.

Each.

Yes, yes. We all know the story by now, don't we, I thought. Must we revisit the vulgar details again?

It seemed I could never escape the reminder of what had happened to my family and me. To others, it was a story to analyze and editorialize in the newspapers I read. The stories that headlined my online feeds. The cocktail party "Did you hear about So-and-So losing his job?" conversation that felt more accusatory than compassionate. One day at a lunch meeting, one of my company's supervisors brought up the fall of a local bank executive before stopping mid-sentence and apologizing to me, a gesture that both comforted and repulsed me, as if I had "Recession Victim" stamped on my forehead.

For the love of John Thain, enough already!

Finally, someone shouted the right answer.

"Bank of America!"

The winner won a book.

I had lost the life I knew and loved.

On the screen was a scriggly graphic of the 2008 Dow Jones Industrial Average. The well-dressed, well-invested speaker gave a crooked smile to the audience.

'This looks like a bad EEG," the well-dressed, well-invested speaker said with another crooked smile. "The market had a seizure."

The audience laughed.

I've never found EEGs funny, especially bad ones belonging to my daughter.

December was overshadowed with fear. By Christmas, I was helping Gilly live with her new normal, adjusting her medicines that either (a) did not work (b) worked, but had side effects, almost sending her with a serious rash to the emergency room or (c) worked too well, reducing the seizures, but making her lethargic, unlike the bright, inquisitive, funny and beautiful girl I loved so much my heart hurt.

Epilepsy treatment wasn't cheap. Christmas giving was tight anyway, with Mike's reduced salary, our stiff IRS monthly payments, bills and out-of-pocket expenses for anti-seizure medicine and tests. One evening during the holiday break, Gilly was having an especially hard time with her latest round of medicine. We were monitoring yet another medicine-induced skin rash that had appeared slowly on her neck. Gilly was restless. Her doctor was on stand-by. So were we.

"Should we take her to the hospital?" I whispered for the tenth time to Mike as we cleaned up after dinner.

"I think we do what the doctor said and give it one more hour to see if the rash spreads," Mike said while he towel-dried a wet dish.

"I told you we shouldn't have started her on the Lamictal," I said. "I had a bad feeling about it after reading the side effect warnings."

"Well, what else could we do?" Mike asked sternly. "Let her have more staring spells?"

"Of course not. Don't be condescending," I snapped and handed him a pot from the sink which I had intentionally left full of water. It spilled all over his cotton shirt.

Mike may have had soapy water on his chest, but I wore resentment everywhere. On my lips. On my heart. On my body, tense and drawn, ready to strike even with a kitchen utensil. I knew this wasn't good for anyone, especially our daughter.

"I'm sorry. This is just so hard," I said, patting Mike's shirt with my dish towel. I grabbed napkins from the counter and wiped my eyes.

Mike took a deep breath and rubbed his shirt. The water spots spread into one large blob, like he'd been hit with a water gun.

"I know," he said motioning toward the TV room, "Let's finish up and cuddle with our babies."

Our babies who weren't infants anymore. Far from it. Our children. Our reason to pull out of our narcissistic selves and be better, braver. And less angry. Maybe it didn't work this way for other parents, but having children brought out the better angels of our nature for Mike and me, although Abe Lincoln probably hadn't said his famous quote after being doused with water by Mary Todd.

"Come here," Mike said, trying to get me to laugh by pulling me into him so I would get wet.

"No! You're drenched!" I laughed, pushing back with my hands on Mike's wet shirt. "Let's go take care of Gilly."

Lying on the couch together, we decided to watch some mindless television in the family room. We often referred to this space as the TV room, but it was more than that. Beside our TV, it housed both Mike and my work space—his small desk, which once had belonged to Griffin, was by the front-facing window and next to my desk on the side wall—as well as our laundry room, my one and only bookcase, and a fireplace that didn't work. Our round black table with four brown and cream fabric chairs was on the opposite side of the room next to the door that led to the pool and garage, so foot traffic was constant. We ate most of our meals here, starting with breakfast and ending with dinner, before finding our favorite spaces on the chocolate brown upholstered couch and love seat to watch television before going to bed.

Flipping the channels while I rubbed Gilly's head, Mike stopped on one featuring cellist Yo Yo Ma. He was playing his latest effort from *The Goat Rodeo Sessions* with a foursome string ensemble playing the oddest and most inviting blend of classical and bluegrass. Yo Yo Ma was the cellist, but there was also a mandolin player in the group. Gilly, the aspiring blue-eyed mandolin player who once wanted to travel the world with her All Star Magic Spirit Band, sat up. Her sallow cheeks turned rosy pink. She began to smile.

A goat rodeo is a polite term used by aviators and others in high risk situations to describe a scenario that requires about one hundred things to go right at once if you intend to walk away from it. Like a plane crash. Or an over-corrected stock market. Or a misfired brain signal.

It was on that night I remembered the familiar sound. The mandolin. "Puckett's Farewell." Where was that CD? Had I sold it? Maybe it was still in the unpacked boxes from too many moves. I also remembered my father/daughter dances after dinner. And my wedding where Coltrane and Hartman introduced a new couple. I remembered Chet Baker and James Taylor and the occasional Michael Buble filtering through in the halls of Oak Lane Cottage.

Oshtroushko's plucky-bell sound serenaded us from our CD player that night as we fell asleep in our burnt orange-painted bedroom where Gilly slept beside us on a spare twin mattress. We'd averted the dangerous medicine-induced rash, but we would have to find a different medicine. For that night, however, we breathed.

On that dark December evening, I had remembered, after the past, stress-induced years of misfired stock markets and brain waves, how much I loved to hear a mandolin weep while being plucked and strummed, even in a cacophony of song that sounded like a goat rodeo.

•   •   •   •   •   •

The new year invited a new resolve to find hope and light in the darkness. I started with a small gesture, listening to music again. The kids and I danced around the kitchen island before dinner. We found a medicine to keep Gilly healthy. Her light-up-the-world laugh returned, especially as we shimmied to some totally rad tunes while cooking.

On one such night, Gilly said, "Hey, Dada, come join us!" and motioned for

Mike to get his boogie on. He was lying propped up on the couch, facing the sliding glass doors to the pool.

"Oh, I think I'll pass, sweetie," Mike said, "I'm a little tired."

He passed on dancing the next evening, too. And the following week, he begged off another restored tradition—nightly walks. By the end of January, Mike could barely stay up past dinner, nodding off by eight o'clock. He was sluggish most of the day. At first I didn't think anything of it. Maybe he was mildly depressed, the weight of Gilly's health and our snail's-pace climb out of debt finally catching up with him. But by February I began to think differently. I encouraged Mike to go to the doctor. A month and a half later, he finally did.

Washing dishes, I looked out the front window as Mike drove into our driveway after reviewing some follow-up tests with a specialist. He sat in the car for a few minutes, not moving.

My cell phone rang.

"Hey, honey."

"Oh, hi, Mama," I said, "Hey, can I call you back. Mike just pulled in and I need to talk to him."

"Well, I was hoping I could see if you could come pick me up," my mother said edgily.

"Well, I can't get you for dinner tonight, but I can pick you up after work tomorrow."

"No, I don't mean for dinner. I want to leave. I don't like it here, Amy," Mom said with her mom voice, like when she had told me I was grounded for a month after I had cut my hair with her sewing scissors when I was in elementary school.

"What?" I asked.

"My roommate is mean and the staff doesn't help out like they should."

Not the best timing for this conversation, I wanted to say, but kept my mouth shut as mom ranted about her "spiteful" roommate who turned the TV up too loud and only watched her murder mystery shows. And the staff was awful, putting mom at a table in the dining hall with women who are "way more sick" and "just plain ugly to one another," mom added.

"You know your daddy would be so upset if he knew his girls put their mama in a nursing home," Mom said and started to cry.

Great. She pulled the "Your daddy" card. Low blow.

"Oh, mama, I know this is a big change for you," I said and glanced out the window to check on my husband, the statue, in his car. "And it's not a nursing home."

"Well, it's not my home!" Mom shouted.

Mike opened his car door.

"Tell you what, I'll pick you up for lunch tomorrow and we can talk about it," I said.

"And all the men here are after only one thing and you know what that is!" Mom said, like a high school teenager.

"Oh, my word, mama! Why don't you get a change of scenery and play cards in the TV room down from your room," I said, trying to change the subject. "I think it is Rummy night and you used to love playing Rummy."

"I don't want to," Mom said defiantly. "I want you girls to get me out of here."

You girls. The four Yeary sisters whose names and lives blurred together, especially when we were in trouble.

"DonnaJulieCindyAmy! You girls get in here right now!" Mama would say after my sisters and I had done something to earn her wrath.

Our front door creaked open as Mike's driveway-gravel embedded shoes tapped on the tiled floor.

"Okay, I promise I'll pick you up for lunch tomorrow, but I'm sorry. I need to go," I said. "I love you, Mama. Try to get some sleep tonight."

As I hung up and Mike walked into the kitchen, his resigned countenance said it all.

"I need surgery," Mike said quietly, first making sure Griffin and Gilly weren't close by.

"It could be thyroid cancer."

I grabbed his face with my hands, locking eyes with him.

"I love you. We will get through this," I said as we hugged in the kitchen, saying nothing more, holding each other so closely that I could feel Mike's warm breath on my neck, chilling me to the bone.

•   •   •   •   •   •

Mike's operation was scheduled the first week of April. My friends Sara and Helen stayed with the children overnight so I could stay in his room after surgery.

"Mike's prognosis seems very encouraging," his surgeon said to me in the hospital's waiting room as Mike was wheeled into recovery. "We'll know what we're dealing with soon, but I think he's going to be just fine."

That night, though groggy from anesthesia, Mike slept well in his hospital room. I slept on a plastic chair that folded out as a bed next to him. *Please let him be okay.* I prayed in staccato pleas over the *beep-beep-beep* of Mike's monitoring equipment.

Please. Please. Please.

By midafternoon the next day, Mike was cleared to go home. No sense in staying in the hospital longer than you have to, his doctor said after stopping by. We will follow up this week, he added, checking the bandages taped across Mike's throat. I helped Mike get dressed, carefully putting on his black linen shirt and khakis. The man was stylish even post-surgery. Wheeling him down the corridor, I noticed everyone was especially kind to him.

"Goodbye," a nurse said bowing her head.

Another nurse smiled as he passed us, holding his hands together like a praying emoji.

"Hello, sir," a white coated doctor said to Mike in the hallway and bowed his head, too.

"Okay, this is weird," I whispered into Mike's ear as I wheeled him into a crowded elevator of patients and medical staff.

"What floor?" A woman asked everyone as the self-appointed elevator caddy.

"Fifth."

"Ground."

"Second."

I was about to answer, when the woman turned toward Mike.

"Father? What floor do you want?"

Father?

Mike and I looked at each other. I bit my lip from laughing. Mike's white bandages were partially concealed by his black shirt, looking as if he were wearing a Catholic vestment like a priest. Mike and I both avoided eye contact so we wouldn't lose it in the elevator.

When we reached the first floor, I quickly pushed Mike out into the lobby where he waved his hands like the Pope to passersby.

"I'll get the car," I said, smiling. "Try not to offer any sacraments while I'm gone."

"And peace be to you," Father Mike chuckled as he motioned the sign of the cross, a blessing we both needed and accepted.

. . . . . .

Mike rested and healed at home. As we waited for his test results, we took comfort that at least we had overcome one hurdle, paying off our IRS debt. Yet forty-eight hours after Mike left the hospital, we found out our volatile financial life—Mike's previous unemployment and Gilly's spike-high medical bills resulting in my withholding too little because we needed every penny we could get—clung to us like the blood-sucking mosquitoes that had returned with Florida's spring rainstorms. Deductions were a figment of our dreams when we didn't own a house. Even renting was a liability. We owed the federal government more than we could pay, once again.

"Five thousand dollars," Mike said, robed in his pajamas with surgical bandages around his neck, after hanging up the phone with our accountant and friend who had graciously assisted us figuring out our income taxes.

"I've seen this happen with individuals in your situation," our friend said. "Too many disincentives and not enough breaks. Makes you stuck in the middle. Let me see if I can work out monthly payments," he added.

Standing in the kitchen in disbelief, we were more than stuck. We just might be sunk. To get out of this vicious cycle, to help my husband heal, to keep my daughter healthy, to care for my mother—who was plotting ways to bust out of her assisted living—to put one foot in front of the other, I would need one hundred things to go right. And quickly.

Chapter 12

The Swimming Pool: Paltry Gear

There I was, holding four swimming pool foam noodles in Target, standing between the aisles at outdoor goods, and I couldn't make a damn decision. I was paralyzed by the pithy choice of should buy all four of the flimsy pool toys (buy one, get one free) or not. A friend had given me a Target gift card for Christmas which I'd forgotten about until now, early April, just in time for the weather to cooperate so Griffin and Gilly could invite friends over for a swim. And just in time for a nice distraction outside the house from what was happening inside.

I thought when the doctor informed us that Mike's thyroid wasn't cancerous, that it was only diseased, and hence removed, the news would be a welcome relief. And it was—my husband was going to be okay, thank God—yet everything else we were facing crushed that ray of hope with a sledgehammer of not-so-fast, missy. I felt like the tired-looking woman in a cartoon with wiry Medusa-like hair and wearing mismatched clothes who said, "I try to take one day at a time, but, lately, several days have attacked me at once."

On top of addressing our new tax problem, mom's housing issue and Gilly's health, we received an email from our landlord saying we either needed to purchase the house by the end of June or he was going to sell it. No more renting. To be fair, Mike and I had signed a lease-option agreement because we were optimistic we'd be in better financial shape to buy the house one year later. After all, we reasoned to each other, we'd have the IRS paid off and could apply that monthly payment to a mortgage. That, plus rent, would more than cover a house payment. And a lease-option usually provided an easier path to buying a house, allowing for a part of the monthly rental to count as a small down payment. This hinged on finding a landlord willing to provide that kind of agreement, and—lucky us!—we found one! We'd finally be homeowners who could build up an asset *and* count deductibles *and* homestead exemption. Take *that*, Mr. Tax Man!

"We could finish the open garage once we buy the house," I said to Mike one day, showing him a picture of a two-car garage in my over-stuffed binder of home renovation ideas. I was a builder's daughter, remember. We can save expenses and do most the work ourselves, I offered.

"I think we could really make the back yard inviting with some landscaping behind the pool," Mike added. "What if we planted a few crepe myrtle trees in the corner by the fence line?"

"Maybe we could add a home office in our bedroom," I said, flipping through my notebook to the home office section. "There's a concrete slab next to the bedroom windows anyway, so that would reduce the cost."

"We need to close in the garage first before adding an office," Mike said.

Yes, that's true, I nodded in agreement. I'll make a note of that on my priority wish list in the front of my binder labeled "Priority Wish List." How clever, Mike chuckled.

After finding out about our tax bill, I realized we were temporarily dwelling in a fantasyland equal to that of the neighboring Disney World where the rides were kiddie-friendly with plastic smiling characters who sang happy songs about small worlds of laughter and a golden sun. Our lives were more like the Twilight Zone's Tower of Terror, located next door from the Magic Kingdom. You can push all the buttons to the top that you want, but you're going down, freefalling like a cable-less elevator. We shared this common plight with many Americans stuck in a rental quagmire. The country's homeownership rate was still falling after the recession, giving a boom in rental revenue to landlords while doing nothing to help renters find a realistic path to buy a home.

It was hard not to resent the situation we were in. We lost our jobs not because we were poor performers, but because the nation's economy tanked. So what did we do? File bankruptcy? Foreclose on our home? Stop paying our bills? None of the above. Four years after the nation and Mangan economic collapse, we were still climbing up a steep cliff trying to grab onto solid financial ground.

We'd found new jobs. Sometimes two at a time. We didn't quit. All of our housing money went to the landlord, none to us and certainly none to be used as a tax credit. We called Gilly and Mike's doctors' offices and hospitals and worked out a structured payment plan for our out-of-pocket medical expenses. Yet we couldn't deduct our medical bills on our taxes. Our loans and debt were paid in monthly installments, including the IRS. At least a monthly mortgage payment had advantageous tax deductions and credits. Renting? Zero.

The real kicker of it all? It was impossible for us to qualify for a mortgage. Cautious lenders had tightened credit standards after the sketchy abuses of the past. Painfully, I had finally come to accept, it was impossible for us to save enough money for a down payment. We weren't veterans, so the zero-down option wasn't available to us. Hell, even federal government-created loans, with smaller down payments, were elusive to us (and most Americans).

We simply didn't possess what was needed to get out of the renting and overly-taxed cycle, no matter how hard we worked our asses off. And because of America's decline in homeownership, that spiked an increase in rentals, thus creating a rental market goldmine with a significant increase in the cost of renting.

No way out.

The weight of moving out of the House of Gray hit my tolerance threshold and rendered me with a debilitating sense of inertia. I couldn't complete even the most mundane of tasks. Like how many pool toys to buy. Or the seeming complexities of grocery shopping (rice or pasta as a side for dinner? Who cared? I bought neither. Or returning personal calls. My cell phone notification message flashed that I needed to delete my voice mail which had reached my limit (I had a limit?). Calling friends back meant talking and talking, meant putting on a positive façade or, worse, not faking it, but instead sharing the latest Mangan tribulations that no one needed to hear, me especially.

Some of my girlfriends tried to coax me out of my funk to join them on their regular social outings, usually drinks and dinner after work. One night I succumbed, thinking it might do me good. I was close with a few of the women, but hesitated as all were financially well-off, or at least to me they were. I had cocooned myself away from friends and acquaintances. But, it was just one night. Live a little. After work I met them at a local trendy restaurant. After a round of Cosmos and salty appetizers, the lips and checkbooks got loose.

"We need to go on another girl's trip," Dawn said, sipping down her martini. "Like the time we went to the Caribbean. Just us girls. No men!"

"Definitely, not the guys," said Sally. "My husband is driving me crazy. And he goes on fishing trips all the time, so I don't feel guilty."

He goes on fishing trips with your son, I wanted to say. I know because Griffin is friends with your boy who talks about his big catches from Islamorada at school. What Mike and Grif would give for father-son fishing trip to the Keys.

"Amy, you should come," another woman at the table urged. "We can stay at a friend's beach house so you'd only have to pay for the flight."

Glancing down at my menu, I focused on the cheapest entrée I could order, thinking a vacation of any kind might be a tad out of my range if I couldn't swing chicken tenders. Yes, Amy, I thought, turning over the laminated menu to the other side with the early bird specials, we know you can't swing it, but come on, girlfriend, you can afford a measly flight ticket, right? That's what they really meant. My stomach churned like the nearby bartender's blender. I was hungry for food and closure of this conversation.

"Or we could use our mountain house in Colorado and go skiing like we did two years ago!" Another Cosmo gal chimed. "Remember when we got stuck on the ski lift and started singing Beyonce? The ski lift operator bought us drinks back at the lodge!"

"Oh, my Gawd, that was hilarious!" laughter erupted around the bar-top table of the Sisterhood of the Traveling Cosmos.

Oh, how funny, I fake-laughed, trying to pivot.

"So, how are your kids doing with end-of-term exams?" I asked knowing no mother can resist talking about her children. Beats travel chatter. "I think it's crazy, the school system schedules testing all in one week's time."

For an awkward pregnant pause, the women stared at me, wide eyed, like I had asked their opinion on the North American Free Trade Agreement.

"Um, Connor doesn't really get test anxiety," said Dawn as she motioned to the waiter for another cocktail.

No, of course not. Silly me. Connor has a private tutor three days a week, I thought.

"I'm more worried about what I'm going to do with the kids all summer," fretted Sally. "Are any of you signing up for camps?"

"I've got mine going to North Carolina for Camp Joy for four weeks, then we're picking them up to take a trip to New York City," said Joni.

"New York City? In the summer?" asked an incredulous and slightly-inebriated Dawn. "It gets as hot as Florida then. We save the city for our annual family Christmas trip for shopping and shows."

"...and ice skating by the Rockefeller Christmas tree," another added.

"Hey, maybe we could do a girls' shopping trip to New York the week after Thanksgiving this year," said Sally.

"Oooooh, I like that idea!" squealed another.

"But, let's not forget about a quick flight to Jan's Bahamas house this summer while the kids are at camp. I need a break," said Sad Sally.

And we were right back to trips. Geeze, it was like watching the Travel Channel. With fruity alcohol.

I managed through the rest of the evening, finally excusing myself by noting I had an early meeting the next day. Driving home, I couldn't wait to walk into the house, throw on my pajamas and cuddle with my family. By the time I opened the front door, I had dialed down my judgment button toward the Girls Night Out group.

They weren't bad human beings. They just happened to live in a vastly different world from me. Different is okay. Several of us had married around the same time, had babies together, secured a first mortgage, scouted for good schools for our expanding brood. Then we ventured into different interests, jobs, lives. When the children would vent about being hurt or disappointed by one of their friends, I'd tell them friendships are often like seasons. We have seasons in our lives and people enter and leave them. A few stay. And those relationships are spectacularly real and raw and true.

And the rest? They're okay, too. Enjoy what you give to each other for the moment before it passes, I'd say. Now it was time for me to heed my own advice. Plus, I'd branched out since starting my job two years ago. Several of my work colleagues had become, wonderfully, real and raw and true friends.

Strangely, my work life was functioning at all cylinders amidst my personal struggles. Neck deep in a long-term company issue impacting one of my communities, I managed the situation with the surprising finesse of a seasoned professional, belying my utility industry inexperience. While only in the business for a year and a half, I responded well to the expectations and challenges, according to my peers, who gave good counsel and constant support. A calming instinct kicked in as though I were possessed with the mind of Warren Buffet and gender-savviness of Cheryl Sandberg. I offered sound professional advice *and* leaned in.

•   •   •   •   •   •

When I got back to the house after my Target trip, four noodles in hand, I found everyone in the pool, Mike, too. An adult needed to be close by Gilly. Swimming is a dangerous risk for epileptics, our doctor repeatedly reminded us. A close friend's epileptic son had almost drowned after seizing in a river. It took three strong-muscled men to pull him out of the river's sandy bottom.

Before Gilly's diagnosis, one of the best parts about living in this house had been relaxing with Gilly in the swimming pool. We were water bugs, sprawling in our bathing suits in the cool water every chance we could get. Mike and Grif didn't take to the pool like we did, and that, Gilly and I laughingly noted, meant we girls had the pool all to our mermaid selves. Even better, we had each other.

So much good is said by the water. Our conversations ebbed and flowed as we sat on the pool's edge, sipping refrigerator-chilled Limonata, thumbing through *People* and *In Style* magazines. Girlfriends, boys, high school drama, aren't-these-shoes-cute-in-this-picture, volleyball, favorite books, colleges, hairstyles, what-can-we-make-for-dinner, Taylor Swift, trendy outfits, movies, Ooh-smell-this-perfume-sample-on-this-page, music, hey, it's time to jump back in the water and cool off.

We especially liked swimming at night. Colorful underwater lights glowed muted yellow, green, blue and red like melted crayons. Sliding beneath the water's surface, we did somersaults through the light beams reflecting off our arms and legs like circus-light spokes on a Ferris wheel. The moon rose to the center of the sky, shining a white hot spotlight over the pool while our fingers and toes shriveled like boiled peanuts after staying in the water for hours on end. We were blissfully water logged.

Now I was miserably afraid to be with Gilly in the pool without Mike.

What if she had a seizure while we were swimming? I wasn't strong enough to pull her out. Just seeing her close to the pool made me queasy.

"Gilly, let's just dangle our feet in the water right now," I said one night by the pool while Mike wasn't there. "Or how about we go for a walk instead?"

"Mama, I'll be okay," Gilly said, frowning by the reminder she was different. Epileptic.

I was different, too. Worry consumed me to the point of ever-present anguish. When Gilly was quiet, I feared she was having a staring spell, temporarily unconscious. When Gilly was at school, I was afraid her teachers wouldn't react quickly enough if she seized longer than a minute. When I had to leave the house before she awoke or went to bed, I wondered, would she take her medicine at the right time? (So I called to double-check. Every. Single. Time.) And what if she missed a dose? And could the medicine have life-long health implications?

And how, I asked, torturing myself in the noisy Hi-Def stereo in my brain, would Mike and I be able to pay another year of monthly IRS payments on top of medical bills and existing structured debt? A big *if,* anyway, since the federal government frowned on repeat payment cycles and was currently reviewing our request.

And what if the historic work issue that I was in the middle of got bigger than I could handle? My company was in the middle of a corporate merger and I knew how that could go. Mike got merged right out of a job, *twice.* Would I lose my job? What would we do if I did?

The depths of my fears had become deeper and darker in the perilous and perverse navigation of keeping my daughter safe and our family solvent. Like the cave divers who dropped into the freshwater caverns of the Silver River near where I lived, my concept of home was constantly redefined. The currents in the river of our lives kept changing, swiftly and furiously. Now we had to move. Third time in four years. More moving expenses, first and last month's rent, security deposit. We were drowning, clutching to anything we could grab, like the flimsy foam pool noodles we used to hang on while splashing and cutting up in the pool of circus lights and illuminated mother-daughter conversations.

This time, I wasn't sure we had what it took to find our way through.

"You will stay on top of the IRS about our payment request, right?" I asked Mike one night. It really wasn't posed as a question.

"I'm on it," Mike responded tersely, leaning down to tie the strings on his running shoes.

"And, since you are at home a lot more than I am, you will stay on top of our budget and make sure we don't underpay again for this current year, right?" I asked insistently, pouring the whole salt shaker into the open wound of perceived past marital omissions.

"Well, I may be home, but I do have a full-time job with a lot of responsibilities, but don't worry, I've got it!" Mike said loudly before slamming the door to go for a run.

Standing there, I was left in my own interrogation puddle of anger and anxiety. After Mike's surgery, my marriage found a gentle place to sublet in both of our hearts. Then the IRS came calling again, reopening a weakly stitched wound and leaving Mike and me reverting to clipped conversations, jabbing here and there when time allowed. And time seldom allowed. Which is why we had stopped talking. Too much required energy. We were too busy surviving.

I hated the bitter push-pull between Mike and me which had resurfaced since we moved out of the apartment. It would come in waves, the marital strife. After all we had been through, I still believed in us as a couple. Listening to some of the women at the restaurant speak so badly of their mates reminded me I had a good one with Mike. No, he wouldn't set the world on fire with a driving ambition. Rather, his drive centered around keeping *our* world, *our* family together. But it troubled me that all this goodness still couldn't overcome the gaps between us.

The past few years showed me I was stronger than I realized. And more flexible, too. I had learned to read the waves better, so I was flapping about all the time. Then, the riptide of another crisis would swell around and pull me under. When I came up for air, I'd often grab onto the float of resentment toward my husband. I wasn't looking for trouble with my marriage, but it was an easy target. Were we equipped as partners to deal with the heavy stuff? You need the right balance of temperament, commitment and desire to keep a marriage together, in the good moments, let alone the times that catapult you into the deep, dark hole of When Bad Things Happen.

While arguing with Mike, I'd missed a phone call. My friend, who was a realtor, said she found a rental half a mile away.

"It's a tri-level and it's four hundred dollars more a month, but there's nothing else available right now," she said on my voice mail. "More people are renting so the market is tighter."

You don't have to tell me that, I thought, holding the phone to my ear. Even our former apartment complex was at full occupancy.

"And it's an older home, but guess what?" she asked in her message, pausing cheerily, "It has a *huge* swimming pool."

PART FIVE: THE TRI-LEVEL

Chapter 13

The Basement: Leaking

Most of my childhood homes were split-level. Dad adored split-level and tri-level, too, and he designed and built multi-tiered houses both for our family and his clients. Wherever we lived, Dad reserved a home office for himself, often tucked away in the back corner of the house, preferably on the top floor with a window facing just below the tree line. His architectural drawing board held the latest house sketch with rolls of other house plans spread across his desk. He wasn't an architect, but often opted to use his plans over those of a certified designer after having to work with "overpaid" architects whom Dad said "had little practical knowledge of what goes into building a house." Could've been a little psychological transference going on.

Dad fancied himself an innovative builder. Every house we lived in, and we lived in plenty, were Sherman Yeary designs, but Dad also kept a sketch of his never-built dream home, a four-level structure with the top floor designated for his office, his builder's version of an executive suite. I'd always found this design style an atypical modernistic choice for a very traditional man. A brick colonial seemed to better fit his conservative personality. But Sherman couldn't help himself. If he could put a kitchen on the floor above the living room and the bedrooms on the floor above the kitchen, he was all in.

"Dad would've loved this," my sister Cindy said after taking a lamp to the top floor of my tri-level house on moving day. She headed down the two-way staircase. "Oh, yeah, this could definitely be a Sherman Yeary design. Look! The family room is in the basement below ground level!"

I peeked around the downstairs corner and saw that she was right. The bottom floor window faced the backyard where the bushes were at eye-level, like we were looking into a terrarium, only we were the ones enclosed. Had I even noticed that before?

Mike and I had quickly toured the house after work at night telling our realtor to send us a rental agreement. We couldn't be picky. Very few places were available in the children's school district. Translation: tighten our money belt that had already run out of notches. Our grocery shopping was like that of a college student's. Ramen noodles. Discretionary spending was nil. Weekends meant free movies on television and pizza with a coupon.

The backyard sloped down and covered half of the house, leaving the other part for a back entrance glass door. One floor up was the dining room, kitchen and front entry and the third floor was reserved for another living space and three bedrooms and two baths. Maybe this would give me some much-needed cardio, I thought, trekking stuff up and down and up and down. Within two hours of unloading, I had lost any paternal sentimental attachment I might have had for the house of many levels.

"I think my heart rate is up," I said with two fingers on my neck, mockingly checking my pulse. "This house may kill me."

Cindy busted out laughing, the familial laugh of a sister who shared my affinity for crushed ice, list making, the beach, day planners, Coca Cola and minimal physical exercise.

"You are going to get a work-out here for sure," she said, wiping beads of sweat off her forehead. "And watch your utility bill. Tri-level houses eat up energy especially at summer time."

How well I knew, having recently shadowed one of my company's energy auditors in a customer's two-story home. Heat rises to the top, she told the homeowners who wondered why their air-conditioner wasn't cooling their home's overly warm second floor. My new rental had *three* stories and a very old air-conditioner that whirred and sputtered in the Florida heat of July. Our top-floor bedrooms were toasty by ten a.m.

"This is not good for a menopausal woman," I said, airing out my sweat-drenched tee shirt. "Let's take a Coke break."

Cindy nodded, but kept unpacking boxes. She was a workhorse, the third-born daughter who could have taken over Dad's building business if she had wanted to. She could build a house. Actually, she *did* build a house—her own— with her husband and Dad helping out during construction, holding up trusses beside awe-struck roofers. Cindy was good at organizing things and people. In another life, she would have made a formidable war-time leader. If Cindy were at

Normandy in World War II, I believe she could've shouldered all the Army Rangers up Pointe du Hoc. Then, she'd have gone back down and straightened up the landing boats.

She was the commander of calm in her baby sister's current universe of chaos.

"Hey, where do you want this bag of clothes?" Julie, Yeary Daughter #2, asked and held up a lumpy white trash bag.

"Can you take it up to my bedroom, please?" I asked and headed toward the refrigerator to fix three glasses of ice cold beverages, a Coke for Cindy and me, and one sweet tea for Julie.

"Oh, crap," I said, opening the freezer devoid of ice. "The ice bin isn't working."

"Add it to your list," Cindy said. After multiple moves, I'd learned to keep a running tab of items that needed repair. By noon, it was disturbingly long.

"Don't worry about it, I ran by Hungry Bear and got us some drinks," Julie said, referencing our favorite local drive-thru whose owners knew the Yeary sisters so well, we had our own accounts there, often paying monthly for our sweet tea, Cherry Cola, twisty fries, Mama Bear burgers and corn nuggets.

Ah, Julie. If Cindy was the commander, Julie was the rescuer. She not only knew when to help, but also knew what essentials to bring, like a Hungry Bear treat, a definite moving day essential.

We three sat on the wood floor sipping the sweet cold nectars of a well-earned break.

"I can't believe you have everything already hung," Julie said, looking at my framed Christmas card collection on the wall.

"She has all her books on the built-in shelves downstairs, too," Cindy added, making me beam a little with pride that my older sisters found something to admire in someone who felt so out of control.

"Well, I've learned it's easier to put up everything before moving in the furniture," I said, opening the lid to my drink to chew on crushed ice.

I may not have had a firm grip on a lot of things, but I had become a damn good mover. Just as with the apartment and the House of Gray, I had developed a system of moving into the tri-level so that by the time the big pieces arrived—the beds, dining room table, buffet and couches—everything else was practically unpacked. I couldn't shake my order-breeds-serenity philosophy even if I tried. For a week before the furniture arrived, I went to the new house after work every night setting up each room, one space at a time.

"Okay, our break is over. What do we need to do now?" The Commander asked and stood up as The Rescuer grabbed our empty cups to put in the trash.

Seeing them in action warmed my heart. I once read a saying "Life made us sisters, love made us friends." True on both counts though I would have added that adversity made us grateful for each other. We'd each had our share of unique difficulties. And while we reveled together when life was smooth, there was something about our shared DNA that elicited a fierce intuitive protection of one another when life got rocky. Just one phone call or text to my sisters announcing my impending departure from my home always evoked the same response from both of them:

"What time do you need me?"

This sibling support system was also a lifesaver in dealing with Mama, who had decided—grudgingly—to give her assisted living facility another chance. For our part, Cindy, Julie and I agreed to adjust our schedules even more to get Mom out and about when she felt up to it. Our solution was a Band-Aid approach on borrowed time, but it was the best we could do at the moment.

"Wait until Mama sees this place," said Julie, "It will remind her of our house on Doris Drive."

"And the one in the country," Cindy added.

"And the one on 10th Street," I laughed.

"What about the one in Stonewood?" Julie asked.

"No," both Cindy and I nodded our heads.

"That was one of Dad's rare one-story houses," I said unpacking a trash bag.

"Yeah, but he also built a tri-level house in that subdivision, too," Julie said. "The Johnson family bought it. I think they still live there."

Looking around my house of many floors, I missed my Daddy. What fun we would have had working on renovation projects here. He was always good at fixing things, too.

Cindy called out from downstairs.

"Hey, add to your list that the guest bathroom toilet doesn't flush well!" Cindy yelled.

Yep, this tri-level was gonna try my patience. It definitely didn't have the Sherman Yeary features of a well-built structure.

• • • • • •

The next morning, I woke up before the sun did with a nagging pressure in my lower abdomen. My back ached, too. Maybe I had pulled a muscle the day before. Mike told me to wait for his help when moving the heavy coffee table. Should've listened to him. The bed's comforter was up to my nose, but I was freezing. It sure as hell wasn't from the air conditioner—that, too, was on the repair list. Did I have a fever?

Not wanting to wake up Mike or the kids, I got out of bed and put on my robe and gingerly walked down the two levels of stairs to our family room in the basement. Every step made my back hurt. Books were my literary Valium so I took one off the shelf, a favorite, Anna Quindlen's *One True Thing*. Pulling a blanket off the couch, I tossed it over my chilled body as I sat down on the side chair and propped up my feet on the matching ottoman.

A burning, pressing sensation overcame me. I rushed to the guest bathroom located on the same floor next to my home office. The bathroom was about the size of a large coat closet with a toilet and pedestal sink with walls painted in a powder baby boy blue. Within seconds, I knew what was wrong with me: I had a bladder infection. A real doozy. I went to the kitchen and poured myself a big glass of water, vowing never, ever to drink another soda in my life, or until the memory of running back and forth to the bathroom had faded. Depositing myself back on the chair, I hoped ole Anna would get my mind off my spastic organ. I began to read, nodding off in blissful Quindlenland.

Then, I had to pee again. Stretching and yawning, I rose from the chair. My socks and the bottom of my pajama slacks felt damp as I stood on the floor. Oh, God. Did I wet my pants while I was sleeping? That's it. No. More. Cokes. Yet, caffeine wasn't the problem. It was the water gushing out of the guest bathroom toilet. By the time I reached the bathroom, the water was flowing into the family room and—horrors!—my home office.

I sloshed through the water to unplug my computer and printer. I waded back into the family room and started lifting the couch and coffee table like I could actually move the furniture outside by myself. Scrap that plan. Racing up to the kitchen, I grabbed a broom from the pantry. Running downstairs, I opened the back door to the garage thinking I could sweep out the water.

Bad idea. The garage was full of unpacked boxes and leftover furniture.

Closing the door, I headed toward the basement door leading to the backyard. Quickly, I started sweeping the water in the direction of the door, but there was too much water in the house. This was more than just a leaky toilet. I turned around and saw Honey standing on the bottom stair, just above sea level. She looked at me like "What the hell?"

"No, Honey! Stay where you are!" I shouted. Honey loved to follow me, especially in the mornings, waking up when I did. The stairwell, where she was perched, was right next to Old Faithful spewing and spitting out its watery contents.

Honey leapt, splashing into the water soaking her paws. I grabbed her and put her on the couch where water was now at its wood base. *One True Thing* floated by. Water was everywhere. Speaking of leaking, I had to pee again. Damn. Honey started to shake uncontrollably like a furry vibrator (she was a Chihuahua-Poodle, a genetic combo inclined to be on the nervous side). I instructed her to stay put on the couch until I returned from using the upstairs bathroom. I felt like Jack saying goodbye to Rose in the *Titanic.*

"Never let go!" I said to Honey, reminding her to stay afloat on the couch.

Wait. I can't leave her I thought. She'd jump down and follow me. I rushed back to pick her up. Just as Honey and I were heading up the stairs, I ran into Mike.

"What happened?" Mike asked looking beyond his frantic, wet wife and dog.

"The toilet is overflowing and it won't stop!" I said and urgently raced past him to find a working bathroom. I put Honey in our bedroom and closed the door. Thank goodness the children were sound sleepers. They'd been up late the night before with the move and Gilly needed her rest before it was time to wake to take her morning meds.

Back in the basement the toilet continued to flow and Mike was trying to sweep out the back door the water that by now had picked up its own faint current.

"Grab some towels!" he yelled while sweeping. I joined him with my broom after throwing all the towels we owned onto the floor. We needed more brooms and sweepers like the magical brooms in *Fantasia's The Sorcerer's Apprentice.*

An hour and a pile of soaked towels later, an emergency plumber arrived, shaking his head, saying the cast iron pipes were clogged with everything imaginable (called it!) and the old pipes really should be replaced.

"I can snake it out this time, but it'll clog again if you're not careful," he said grumpily.

Uh-huh. How exactly does one be careful when using the toilet, I wondered.

"One more thing," he said as he walked toward his truck, "I'm going to be working on the pipes so hold off using the toilets for a while."

Oh, sure. It's not like I'm dealing with a hyperactive bladder convulsing like an accordion played by a street vendor on crystal meth. I'll ignore the three quarts of water I just consumed, too. No problem!

My phone alarm buzzed. Gilly needed to wake up and take her anti-seizure medicine. She had her medicine alarm, too, so mine served as back up. I heard feet shuffling upstairs. Good, she's up. While Mike picked up sopping wet towels from our floors to put in the dryer, I decided to surprise Gilly and Griffin with breakfast in bed. Let's turn this frown of a day upside down!

Except for one thing. There was nothing in the pantry that was breakfast-worthy unless I could convince the kids canned spinach and pinto beans were optimal choices.

The day before we were so busy moving we forgot to go to the grocery store. Clothed in a sweatshirt and sweatpants on a summer morning, I developed a feverish chill. I wanted nothing more than to make breakfast for the kids and then fall into my bed after running an I.V. line of major antibiotics directly into my veins to knock out the now raging urinary tract infection I was certain I had. I did not, however, feel up to making a grocery-store run for breakfast, but a mother's gotta do what a mother's gotta do. Just as I headed upstairs to get my purse, the doorbell rang. Alright! I won't use the damn toilet! I thought as I opened the door, expecting to be greeted by the plumber bearing more bad news about my clogged pipes.

"Hello!"

It was my friend, Julee, who lived close by, holding a basket of homemade muffins, blackberry jam and oranges.

"I thought you might like something for breakfast on your first morning in your house," she said, smiling.

I hugged her tightly, trying not to cry or pee.

·　　·　　·　　·　　·　　·

Floridians are inherently optimistic about the weather. In spite of hurricanes, thunderstorms and heat waves, we plug along happily at the notion there exists a season where none of the above occur. Also known as Fall and Winter. We residents of the sunshine state pull out our barely-worn winter coats when the weather is chilly, which lasts about two whole weeks in the middle of January.

There was another season upon me, Griffin's senior year in high school. As he blew out eighteen candles on his chocolate cake one October evening, I could already see him walking in June across the graduation dais accepting his diploma. While he laughed with friends surrounding him as he opened the presents they'd brought him, I wondered if there was a policy against mothers living with their children in college dorms.

College. I wasn't ready. I thought I would be, but I found myself walking around daydreaming about having one more year at home with my son. Just one more. Then I'd be ready. Maybe it had something to do with the fact that every single year of Griffin's high school career involved us moving from one place to the next. And staying ahead of the unemployment line and the IRS and aging parents and misbehaving brains and thyroids. Guiltily, I worried if Mike and I had parented Griffin with enough attention, love and discipline to prepare him for this next big chapter in his life.

Then I looked at him. He was quietly confident, brimming with an intellectual curiosity that made him keenly articulate about causes that mattered to him. He zeroed in on the needs of the poor and underserved and helped Mike with food drives at his school for the homeless shelter. This led him to want to know more about the policies that influence the social issues of our time. He sailed through advanced classes in philosophy, ethics and comparative politics.

Music was a constant, too, as Griffin honed his guitar skills both on acoustic and electric as crisp, melodic tones echoed from his room. For me, one of the most rewarding parts about being a parent was watching my children evolve into their young adult personhoods like human math equations as they added and subtracted passions, skills and relationships to arrive at a this-feels-right-for-now solution.

Griffin was ready for college. Like it or not, I needed to be, too. But just a few more *West Wing* television marathon nights on Netflix were in order for my boy and me, our favorite mother-son tradition next to our family's Saturday nights at Barnes & Noble. Griffin's first choice was Florida State University located in

Tallahassee, our state's capitol, thus the hub for strong university programs in political science and international affairs, two of Griffin's desired majors. He heard about the university's Living and Learning Community that offered freshman year dormitory living with emphasis on areas of interest for students of like mind and major. So he applied for the Social Justice Living and Learning Community Program that required more paperwork and an essay.

One Saturday Griffin walked into my basement home office where I was sitting in front of my computer.

"Hey, Mom, do you mind printing a copy of my essay to FSU?" Griffin asked. "I sent it to you as an email attachment."

"Sure thing," I said closing my laptop document so I could find his email.

As Griffin stood over me at my chair, a dark shadow dashed passed the corner of my eye. It was a black spider the size of my hand, with long spindly legs and a large black sac like it had swallowed a golf ball.

"Ahhhhh!" I screamed and almost tipped over my chair as it ran across my foot before resting on the floor beneath my desk. Griffin backed up and ran to get something or someone. I was hoping he'd bring back a hammer or a professional exterminator. He returned with Mike and a can of wasp spray.

Good enough.

Mike first tried to smash the spider with his shoe, but that sucker was lightning fast, scurrying back and forth on the floor. Gilly walked in to see what the commotion was about.

"Hey, what's going...ahhhhh!" she screamed when she saw the spider.

Now, as optimistic as we Floridians are about our weather, we are equally accepting of the critters that inhabit our sub-tropic state. Alligators, snakes and bugs of all kinds co-exist generally with the rest of us, including spiders of all kinds. But this spider was creeping us out with its bulging belly and legs that seemed to be growing larger in front of us. And the tri-level seemed to posses every native species of spiders. In the kitchen. On the ceiling in the family room. In the— dear Lord!—shower. And now, here in my one and only private space. I might never set foot in it again, I said to myself, as Mike was intently playing whack a spider by my chair.

"Gimme the can!" Mike said to Griffin, who handed him the wasp spray like a surgeon's assistant.

With his finger on the nozzle, Mike targeted our creepy crawler. As the spray hit its body, the spider tried to move, its legs expanding in and out.

Then, it happened.

The spider's bulbous sac exploded and hundreds of baby spiders spilled out of it and spread out in all directions, covering the white tiled floor like black ink pellets.

"Ahhhgggggggghhhhhhggggghhh!" We all screamed, bolting out of the door except for Mike, who started machine gun spraying the spiders like he was in a Quentin Tarantino film.

After he had successfully drowned our invaders, the basement reeked of bug spray.

"Let's get out here," I said to my family as they held their noses.

"Where do you want to go?" Mike asked with a knowing grin. Hey, it was Saturday and that meant a trip to the bookstore where we almost always ended up after dinner. Sure, it was a tad early for our regular jaunt, but why not?

"Wanna get lost in Barnes & Noble?" I said, our favorite family catch-phrase of all time. Nothing beat losing ourselves in the aisles of a bookstore...together.

"Yes!" both Griffin and Gilly said in unison, eagerly ready to leave our spider-infested house.

"What else does this house possess?" I said, shaking my head to Mike as the kids ran upstairs to get ready for the bookstore.

Mike shook his head. The house was getting to him, too. Not an easy feat for my steady husband.

"Well, less a few hundred spiders," he said wiping the basement floor of the residue of the unwelcome.

·   ·   ·   ·   ·   ·

Many may deny it, but parents live vicariously through their children. I was no exception. Oh, if I could rewind the hands of time and broaden my options for college like Griffin, who had chosen his college based on his passion. Me? My friends. And played volleyball like Gilly. Me? Assistant track coach, a position created by the high school coach once he realized I couldn't even make the freshman stay-at-home-on-tournament-day track team, a major disappointment to Dad, a high school track star. (Thank you, Coach Robbins, for your pity. I loved every minute of clocking the runners at practice.)

So that's partially why I jumped into supporting what had become a major volleyball movement in Marion County which had resulted in Gilly's team winning the county's first high school state championship. Most importantly, Gilly loved the game, feeling normal and competitive in front of the net with her teammates who cared for her on and off the varnished court gym. Her volleyball team, their families and her coach carried us during the dark days of Gilly's diagnosis, insisting she was a valued member of the varsity team, a group of stand-out girls, smart, athletic and kind. And for that, I loved them with every fiber of my jiggly body.

Gilly's sweet sixteenth birthday was especially sweet when her team brought home the state championship trophy. After the out-of-town tournament victory, our caravan of tired-but-excited girls and parents pulled into the Ocala Ale House around nine p.m. with a crowd of locals waiting for us before breaking into a chorus of "Happy Birthday" to Gilly.

The celebration continued on the weekend with a bonfire in our backyard by the swimming pool none of us had used the previous summer. As Gilly's volleyball team and friends sang Katy Perry and One Direction at the top of their lungs while roasting marshmallows in the fire, Griffin and I retired to the basement family room. Close to midnight, the party hanger-on's carried the party to Gilly's bedroom. Tired from a few action-packed days, I locked the back door after dumping a cooler of ice outside. Bedtime was just within my reach.

"Hey, wanna watch West Wing?" Griffin asked, my son who would leave me for his freshman summer term in college nine months later.

I looked at my watch. Then at him.

"Heck, yeah," I said, finding a comfy spot on the couch next to Griffin as the show's sweeping orchestral score began. Gently, I held his hand as the night turned into a new day.

Chapter 14

His Room: Letter from a Young Lad's Mother

On rare occasions, I found myself alone in the house after my tribe left for the day and before I headed to work. This came to be one of my favorite alone moments. Sometimes, I'd walk around the house, lost in thought, picking up discarded newspapers and laundry. One morning, I returned an errant sock to Griffin's room. That's when it hit me, that Griffin would be in college this time next year, somewhere else, and not here. What a lucky college, I thought. So, I wrote a letter to the university, a letter I never sent, but considered suggesting a new admissions component that included letters from mothers. No one would be required to read them, but I bet it would make a ton of moms feel better about the process.

Fall 2012

University Admissions Officer
University of Griffin's Choice
Far Away from Mom, USA

Dear Admissions Officer,

I'm in my son's bedroom as I write this letter, sitting on his twin bed, the one his father slept in as a young boy and the one my son has insisted on keeping even though it's old, rickety and small. Like Game of Thrones' Peter Dinklage small. But Griffin loves it. He's always been sentimental. On his dresser sits a ceramic bowl of gray river stones. Wedged in between them is a wallet-sized photo of a dear family friend, Steamboat, who lost his life to cancer.
So this is Griffin.
Griffin Patrick Mangan, first born, first loved, first everything really. First time I knew what complete surrender to love felt like. Even his entry into the

world was extraordinary. He was born two months prematurely, contracted meningitis, spent forty-two days in a teaching hospital's neonatal unit, weighed three pounds, and showed everyone he was a fierce preemie warrior from the start, a "fine wee little man" his Scottish-born neonatologist said.

But I digress. I've been doing that a lot lately—getting sidetracked in the scrapbook of my heart, focusing too long on snapshots of memories of my son who has grown into a grounded and gracious young adult. Which brings me to you. Apparently, Griffin is old enough to consider college. I must have overslept one morning and woke up to find my four-year-old boy who loved Tonka trucks and Legos in equal measure had turned eighteen. Eighteen.

And now he's applied for acceptance into your fine university. Your liberal arts program complements Griffin's inclination toward the broad view of humanity. He gets it. And what he doesn't understand, he seeks to comprehend in his own sentient way. I swear I'm not saying this because I'm his mother. See for yourself with Griffin's college application that he completed on his dad's laptop, our only family computer throughout Griffin's high school years.

Which brings me to what Griffin wrote to you in his college entrance essay. Why he said he was especially interested in the concept of social justice, of helping others. Why I cried the first time he showed it to me. He doesn't have his own computer. That in itself isn't a big deal, really. But he also doesn't possess a lot of the things that do matter, and that our family once took for granted—financial security, the same place to live longer than a year, steady jobs for mom and dad and, especially, good health for his little sister Gillian. We've been swept up in a tornado of turmoil and uncertainty, tossed and spit out as collateral debris. Through all of this, however, Griffin has never given Mike and me that petulant comeuppance teenage attitude of "Why me?" when others had a life that his family and he did not.

Instead, as you'll read in his essay, Griffin asks "Why does this happen at all?" He's told me he'd like to learn from your faculty and fellow students how social policy influences societal outcomes. And how he can help. How he can make a difference to help those who get caught in the path of pain and loss. And he means it. And not just because it sounds good enough to be placed on top of the list of worthy college applicants. Look, even if you deny admission to Griffin, even if he doesn't get enough scholarship dollars, he will still find a way to make his altruistic mark, carve out a meaningful life. I love this kid. Okay, he's not a kid *anymore.*

Hanging out alone in my son's room isn't the best idea for someone wallowing in motherly moroseness. Yet, here I am, somberly staring at Griffin's bulletin board of thumb-tacked photos of friends, Gillian, Mike and me, and the rattle from a snake that his late Uncle Joel gave to him. On the wall hangs his electric and acoustic guitars, gifts from kind-hearted friends who saw musical potential in Griffin. I wonder if he'll take them to college. Maybe if Griffin keeps them here, he will visit more often. And I refuse to walk into his closet that holds his now-retired Air-Soft gun and two large trash bags of Legos he can't seem to part with. (Don't ask about the trash bags. It's a Mangan thing.)

There's a tiny book of poetry on Griffin's dresser next to his bowl of rocks that belonged to "Papa," my late father and Griffin's beloved grandfather, who read aloud with him the classics like Call of the Wild *and* Robinson Crusoe. *Papa loved poetry, too. He was fond of the Scottish Poet Robert Burns, whom he'd often quote. Actually, he quoted the same poem again and again, usually to me after dinner—Burns'* Epistle to a Young Friend—*of "young lads" seeking an independent life of their own with a good measure of prudence. Dad brought a book of Burns' poetry back as a souvenir from a trip to Scotland. It is covered in a Tartan green, red and blue fabric and is the size of a measuring tape, perfect if you are a Lilliputian. Griffin assumed ownership rights of the book after Dad died. A wee little book for a wee little man.*

Oh, gosh, here come the waterworks! I think it's best I leave his room now.

Here's the thing about Griffin and your university. You'll miss out on an exceptional young man if you don't accept him. And I will lose a part of me if you do. Which, I believe, is exactly how it's supposed to be if we're lucky enough to love so bone-marrow deeply that you mourn for the memories, weep for the trials and cry for the joy at the chance to witness a new life evolving right in front of you.

Most sincerely,
Griffin's Mom
P.S. Do you offer guest lodging that connects to the dorms? Just curious.

Chapter 15

The Neighborhood: Pieces of Me

If you don't want reminders of your past, don't hold a garage sale. And if you must, leave town. Five years after moving out of Oak Lane Cottage, I kept bumping into furniture I once owned. Like the time Mike, Griffin, Gillian and I were invited to dinner at the home of a girl whom Griffin was dating and found my grandmother's oak table—the one that had served as my desk in Oak Lane's library—in the family's screened-in porch. The top had been painted a pale gray, but it was definitely Granny's table. I'd know those spindle post legs anywhere (the table, not Granny's).

Griffin and Gilly were eating dinner with his girlfriend and her brother when I walked in, instantly recognizing the table and weirding out like it was an ex-boyfriend.

"Um, I think this used to be our table," I said, trying to process why the table was there. "But, I mean, no big deal. We ended on good terms. I'm glad you're together now."

Turns out Girlfriend's family was friends with friends of ours who bought the table at our garage sale, but ended up not wanting it, so gave it away.

There was also the time I picked up Gilly from a slumber party. I followed her into the master bedroom where her friend's mom had piled all the sleeping bags on the king-sized bed that looked an awful lot like the black wrought iron bed in our master bedroom at Oak Lane because it *was* our bed. Same garage sale.

And the black-lacquered side table, which welcomed visitors in my home's foyer with seasonal displays of wooden pumpkins and scented pinecones, now greeted me in the entryway of someone else's home when I arrived for a dinner party. It seemed as though everywhere I went, another Mangan relic stood waiting for me, my own antiques road show.

The tour went beyond the city limits. One day at work, I was shadowing Bill, an engineer in Gilchrist County, two counties north of Marion County. We knew each other outside of work. His wife's parents grew up with mom and dad in Ocala. After lunch, Bill took me on a ride-a-long to show me our distribution grid.

"Hey, Cathy asked me to swing by the house so she can see you for a minute," Bill said as he put on his blinker at a four-way stop.

Pulling into his driveway, Cathy walked out of the house smiling. We visited for a few minutes, catching up. While Cathy and I caught up, Bill walked into his work shed next to the house. He was a skilled woodworker and novice builder who, earlier that day, told me how dad had been a mentor to him. When he returned, he was holding something rather large behind his back.

"I have something for you," he said with a sheepish grin. "Cathy's dad somehow ended up with this and gave it to me knowing how much I thought of Sherman."

There it was. Dad's drawing board.

Memories overcame me. I was twelve again sitting on my Sears & Roebuck white canopy bed, knees propped with the polished blonde-wood board perched on my lap as I sketched designs for my bedroom, thrilled dad let me borrow his drawing board to pursue my love of home design. I was nineteen in college, having recently discovered a passion for history and chatting with dad in his home office about the significance of Great Britain's alliance with America during World War II. Architectural renderings of his tri-level dream house were scattered on top of his drawing board at his desk. I was a young mom picking up Griffin and Gilly from a fun night at Mama's and Papa's as they excitedly handed me pencil-drawn pictures of trees and houses and flowers they drew on one of Papa's sketch pads while sitting in front of his drawing board.

"I'm going to be a builder like Papa!" Gilly said and handed me her picture.

Papa. Sweet Papa.

Dad.

Sherman Yeary.

I swear he was standing next to me on that asphalt driveway in Trenton, Florida, of all places, as I held his drawing board, running my fingers across the still-smooth wood. Mama must have given it to Cathy's dad when he was still alive. I had asked Mama repeatedly what happened to it, but she didn't remember and it made me mad as all get-out how she could lose something so special, not realizing she was losing her memory.

"Your dad would want you to have this." Bill said. "He always bragged about you being his little builder."

Misty-eyed, I hugged Bill and Cathy who understood what this meant to me. When we were back in Bill's truck, I kept dad's drawing board securely on my lap as we passed fields blanketed with green-leafed rows of ripe peanuts like the kind dad and I would buy at a boiled peanut stand on the side of the road on our way to University of Florida football games. Gingerly holding the damp, hot brown bag, I'd "peel and pass" as dad joked, handing him salty, shriveled peanuts while he drove and we listened to the football pre-game radio show.

"Maybe this will be our year the Gators will win it all," Dad said optimistically as he popped a peanut in his mouth. He was always optimistic about his beloved Florida Gators, in good seasons and bad. "What do you think, honey?"

"I think so, too, daddy," I said, not really knowing a thing about college sports, only knowing there was no where else I'd rather be than with my father in his truck heading to a football game, to a construction site, to anywhere.

And now I had a piece of him, returned to me for safekeeping that I vowed to keep forever.

· · · · · ·

On the day of Griffin's high school graduation party, a hot Saturday in June, the old air-conditioning system in our sparsely insulated, tri-level home wasn't up for a celebration. By 11:00 a.m., the thermostat topped eighty degrees—*inside*.

"People won't stay long if it gets any hotter," I said to Mike, fanning myself with a paper plate as I laid out napkins and plates next to the tray of ham and turkey sandwiches on the dining room table.

"I don't know what you want me to do about it. The air conditioner needs to be replaced," Mike said testily as he walked downstairs with a cooler of ice.

I want you to fix it, I thought. Not the air conditioner or the insulation or the leaky toilet or the broken pool pump. Or the other twenty things wrong with this rental. I want you to fix *us*. Make us better, settled. Whole. Not broken into little pieces, reacting to the world rather than shaping it into a life we desire.

Sure, I could do my part to keep us together. Matter of fact, that was my one constant. But there had to be some give and take. I felt like the ants in the ant pile outside our front door, scurrying in all directions when sprayed with repellant and then rebuilding another home until the next poisonous rain hit. And I was the ant saying "Don't you think we should re-consider this whole living arrangement?"

Griffin's high school graduation reminded me just how unsettled we were. He was accepted into F.S.U.'s social justice living and learning community and would begin the summer semester two weeks after graduation. At a time when I should have been celebrating his accomplishments, I found myself burdened with worry and regret. My son was leaving home for college. On top of the typical motherly worries—Is he ready? Am I ready?—I struggled with a deeper regret. Were Griffin's high school years hijacked by our mercurial circumstances?

The moment I had seen that little blue line appear into view in the pregnancy test wand, I began dreaming of the life I wanted for my child. Eighteen years later, I had some unfinished business on the list. Big and small stuff. I wanted to show him the Grand Canyon, the vastness of the earth beyond Ocala, Florida. And send him to music camp, growing his talent among peers. Grif would have loved that. And more family beach vacations. He was ten the last time we dug our toes in the sand at our favorite condo in St. Augustine. And we were only on season three of *West Wing*. It wasn't my fault there were so many episodes in a season, right? I was busy. And tired. My bed beckoned me at the end of each work day that often began before the sun rose.

Most days and nights, my head was full of worry and fear that I couldn't turn off. Even when I was with Griffin, my mind was racing somewhere else. Did I set the alarm to leave early for my work trip? Should I reply to one more email before I go to bed? What bills can we pay before our next paycheck? How can we save enough to stop this renting cycle and buy a house? Did I return that customer's call? Remember to tell Mike about a job I heard about. And on and on.

What did I have to show for it? More importantly, what did Griffin see? God, I hoped he saw a mother who loved him. I hoped he *felt* it. In everything and everywhere. But, I wasn't sure. How could I be? I had been so preoccupied with keeping my family secure for so long that I feared I had stopped being present and lost the very piece of me that I wanted Griffin to have with him wherever he went.

A year before dad died, he and mom surprised my three sisters and me by taking us to lunch and then informing us they had plans for a very special dessert. They drove us to our first home, a split-level, fittingly. The house was for sale and mom had a key since she was a realtor. We walked around the empty house for half an hour, recounting funny family stories that every room held. Dad started to share another story, then caught himself tearing up and so did we.

Would Griffin have enough of the good part of our story to carry him on his journey to independence? Did Mike and I do right by him? So often Griffin would share a favorite memory from his childhood, usually connected to where he was living at the time. Driving his battery-operated car at our first home. Lining up his *Star Wars* Legos on the wood floor of his upstairs bedroom at Oak Lane and creating imaginary battle scenes until bedtime. Playing Scattegories and Trivial Pursuit at Christmas in our apartment. Strumming the Beatles on his acoustic guitar in his room at the House of Gray. *West Wing* marathons with mom at the tri-level. These were the stories he said he remembered.

Please, let this be sufficient, I would pray. Then the money demon would jump on my shoulder and poke me with his pitchfork, asking, "Memories don't pay for college. What are you going to do?"

Good question. Griffin's scholarships would help. So would my job. And Mike's. But it wouldn't be enough. Our expensive rental with a through-the-roof monthly utility bill was a big financial drag. We'd easily save eight hundred dollars if we found somewhere else to live. Which is why we could not stay in the tri-level, why we would move into a cheaper rental two weeks after Griffin's move to Tallahassee, our fifth home in five years, why our move would be exactly one year since the last time we pulled out the packing boxes.

.   .   .   .   .   .

"Mom, they're here," Griffin said as the doorbell rang with guests ready to celebrate my son's rite of passage. Dressed in a blue button-down shirt and khakis, he was wearing his thick, black hair longer, like Paul McCartney or a boy about to go off to college.

"Are you ready?" he asked walking toward the entryway past the kitchen.

Wiping beads of sweat off my brow, I pulled out the tray of cookies I had made. There was a melted, abstract swirl of garnet and gold in place of the "FSU" I had intended to spell, but it was the best I could do.

"As ready as I'll ever be," I said giving my high school grad a quick hug before opening the door.

Hours after the party, after we had cleaned up, after Griffin and Gilly had found a movie to watch together, Mike and I decided to take a walk. Like the duck whispering apartment days of our past, we needed to talk in private. We had put off this conversation until after Griffin's graduation, or, rather, I had put it off until then. Mike was seldom one to broach discussing the serious matters of our marriage where I was all Oprah when I believed I needed to be.

Let's go this way, I said, gesturing toward the street corner as we closed the front door. For a few minutes we walked in silence, numbed by Griffin's big day and the festivities that followed. This was a familiar route, our old neighborhood. We knew most of our neighbors. Mrs. Johnston's water oak tree still needed trimming from the last time we resided in this area of the city, called "Woodfields" for the stately oak and pine trees that dwelled beside rows of seventies era-built houses with overbuilt new construction homes wedged in between them.

"I hear E.L. had surgery," Mike said as we passed the one-story house of the former mayor who, at Halloween, would greet our neighborhood crew of costumed children with copious amounts of candy while disbursing miniature bottles of wine for appreciative parents.

"I like the new addition the Cauthens built," I said as we walked a little farther, realizing the residential landscape had changed in Woodfields since the last time we lived there.

"I always thought that house had potential," Mike chimed in before we crossed a busy street.

"This one, too," I said, pointing to a house for sale. "Just needs some paint and landscaping."

"Maybe add a garage," Mike said.

We could've done this all night long, renovate houses we'd never own. In some ways this was Mike and I at our best, coming together in fervent hope we could forget our differences for a while to fantasize about house additions, paved driveways and enclosed garages. We'd been together for over twenty-four years, married for twenty-three. I discovered marriage was a lot like the movie *Groundhog Day,* with many days being the same. Same conversations, habits, meals, errands, grocery store list, nighttime ritual (each reading our book of the moment before nodding to sleep, me first, usually). The mundane often leads couples to find spontaneity in destructive ways—infidelity, addiction, leading separate lives—yet, for Mike and me, it's what grounded us. After all we had been through, we embraced the notion of sameness.

And yet.

There was one pervasive reoccurrence I simply could not stomach, one more move driven by uncertainty about our future. This time had to be different. No more "it's an adventure!" that I would cheerily tell anyone while wrapping Wedgwood china in bubble wrap, my teeth clenched a little too tightly. Screw adventure. Give me banality.

I didn't naïvely think Mike and I wouldn't face our share of struggles. I just didn't expect there to be so many of them. Right or wrong, marriages are often defined more by the challenges than the victories. Which is why I tried so damn hard to swim in our successes. We were still together, our children were doing well, Gilly was stable, we both had jobs. Almost daily, I'd mentally review my gratitude list to pivot toward the light, not the darkness.

However, my innate desire to find order and purpose coupled with Mike's approach to dwell in the present, his "let's just hunker down and get through this" response to life, created a dissonance that divided us. For many years, I tried to convince myself our differences complemented who we were as a couple while allowing us the individuality any relationship needs to survive. But facing another move to another rental to another part of town on top of ever-present financial insecurity made me question if surviving was enough. I needed more than that. And Mike deserved that as well.

"Mike, I'm not sure I can keep doing this," I said quietly as we walked.

"Well, I hope this is our last move for a while," Mike said. "I think a lease option for this next house will give us a chance to own a home."

"But I'm not even sure if this is the home I want to buy. And, realistically, I don't see how we can with Griffin in college," I said.

"What do you want me to do then? You keep saying we need to stop renting. So this could be a solution," Mike said as his voice elevated in urgency.

"First, I want you to stop asking me what I want you to do. Don't you know by now?" I asked, tired of the rhetorical responses Mike often gave. "We're reacting again. We have to leave this rental, it doesn't make sense to stay, but because we still don't have a plan with goals lasting longer than our noses, we're falling into what's convenient."

"You found the house. Now you don't want it?" Mike asked testily.

"It's not about the house. It's about us," I said hesitantly. "I'm not sure I can keep doing this...*us.*"

Mike shook his head in silence as we turned a corner toward the Smith house we'd always admired for its red-brick traditional design.

"Hello?" I asked and nudged my husband to respond.

"Look, we've been through a lot. And we're making progress. It's going to be tough with Griffin in college, but I'm working hard at my job and I know you are, too," Mike said looking straight ahead at the road in front of him. He heard me, but he wasn't listening.

"So what happens a year from now? Two years from now when Gilly starts college?" I asked urgently. "What's our plan?"

"We're going to keep doing what we're doing now. We're paying down our debt. The IRS will be paid off. Hopefully, I can get a raise and..." Mike said before I cut him off.

"Yes, but your job doesn't offer any long-term security. No benefits, retirement. And you're not getting any younger. I feel like it's all on me to plan for our future," I said, repeating a statement I'd made before. "I've begged you to help me put some steps in action so we have identifiable goals and ways to reach them. I don't believe I'm asking for anything extraordinary. And you've asked a lot of me. I've made sacrifices to save our family."

"We both have," Mike said curtly, accelerating the pace of his walk as if to get the hell away from me.

And I welcomed the distance, tired of the way our recent conversations increasingly digressed into an argument without a solution. I didn't believe I was asking for anything more than what our family deserved. But it was as though Mike and I were speaking different languages, unable to interpret one another's intentions. And what was my intention? Simply not to repeat the past. The future scared me, but the thought of finding myself one year from now in the same position I was in on this night frightened me to my core.

Catching up with Mike, I broached a subject weighing heavily on my exhausted heart. Divorce. And I wondered if this is how it begins? The start of the end of a marriage. One spouse, or maybe both, end up so tired of fighting the battle, that they lay down their lances and walk away from the trench. I'd long surpassed the anger phase. The daily struggles had weakened my resolve. A wise older woman had once told me "The key to a successful marriage is not wanting to divorce on the same day."

I knew Mike would not initiate this consideration. He was the one looking down while walking, as I stared straight ahead, looking for the right path. And here was the kicker of it all. I still loved him deeply. But I did not see how we could continue as a couple if we both weren't committed to making real changes in our relationship. I believed his passive and my aggressive (or reactive and proactive, as I chose to see it) would eventually destroy our family. How odd, I thought, that I loved him and my family enough to think about ending it before we were all decimated. Marital death by a butter knife.

"Maybe we should think about you moving to an apartment when the kids and I move to the house," I said, launching the grenade.

Mike continued walking, his head bowed.

"Is that what you want?" he asked, once again, putting the onus on me.

"I don't know how to tell you any differently than what I keep saying that I want for all of us," I said, my voice breaking. "Why can't you help me?"

"I *am* helping, Amy," Mike said, enunciating my name in a sharp syllabic tone. "But, if that's what you want..."

"Damn it, Mike. I want you to care enough to help save us. I honestly believe if I said for you to move out, you would because it's easier than to stay and fight for us," I said, my voice raised as we passed the McAllister's house with the backyard fort where the kids used to play.

"That's not true," Mike said, his eyes turning into angry slits.

And there we were at an impasse, the purgatory of marital discord, neither one of us able to escape our mutual convictions and complexities. We walked a few more blocks in tepid solitude until we reached another intersection, one we had avoided for five years.

Oak Lane Cottage.

The Cape Cod house peeked behind the grand oak tree in the front yard as Mike and I realized that while we had been so consumed in arguing about our future, we had run smack into our past.

"Let's turn around," Mike said hurriedly when he saw our former home. At first I had the same inclination, but I couldn't stop walking toward Oak Lane, drawn to the magnetic pull the house still had over me.

"No, it's okay," I said, slowing down my pace as we reached the corner of the yard, the spot where Mike gave me a white-painted trellis one Mother's Day, where it still stood, though it needed a white-wash.

Drawing closer to the house, my heart was racing like the hummingbirds that

I saw crisscrossing its backyard. Only one car was in the driveway, leading me to hope no one was home to see us walking by. Just as we reached the mailbox, I noticed a large object placed next to it. A piece of furniture, the top turned over onto the grass with its four wood legs straight up like rigor mortis had set in. I recognized it instantly.

It was my dark-stained side table that mom passed down to me.

The table that was with me from my first apartment to the last home I owned.

The table Griffin and Gilly played chess on. Ate endless bowls of mint chocolate chip ice cream on.

The table I later moved next to our family room sofa and love seat to serve as the perfect place for my new lamp.

The table I reluctantly agreed to include in the sale of the house at the owner's request. I wouldn't have room for it in our apartment anyway, I rationalized.

"Oh, my God," I gasped. "It's my table!"

"Awwww," Mike said. "I'm so sorry. I know you loved that table."

"Why toss it on the curb? I would have taken it back," I said, acting as if I still had ownership rights to it.

"I don't know," Mike said as we both stood next to the table, unsure what to do, staring down at it like it was a wounded animal. Headlights shined behind us. A truck was approaching.

"Should I ask them to hold onto it until we can come back and pick it up?" I asked.

"Let's just walk back to the house and I'll get the car to come back," Mike said gently.

"But it may not be here by then," I said.

"It will be if we hurry. Who knows how long it has been here," Mike said, gesturing for us to resume walking. "Besides, I don't think anyone is home to ask."

"What if that truck picks it up?" I asked.

"Come on, let's go. I'll come back," Mike said.

We quickly walked back to our rental, not saying much, both lost in thought. When we reached our garage, Mike rushed inside and returned with his car keys. As he pulled out of the garage, I stood in the driveway, overcome by finding another piece of me. Another reminder I was scattered all over the damn place. I mean, honestly. It had been five years. The furniture road show should have ended by now.

I bent down, my hands on my knees. Breathing in. Breathing out. It's just a stupid table, I thought, swallowing the burning reflux of regret. I stayed outside until Mike returned. Pulling into the driveway, Mike rolled his window down as I saw his closed trunk.

"I'm sorry," he said. "When I went back, it was already gone."

Biting my bottom lip, I refused to cry. How could I mourn something I gave away?

"That's okay," I said, walking away from him. "I'm sure I'll run into it again someday."

PART SIX: PARK VIEW

Chapter 16

The Closet: A Dog, A Crow and Ashamed

This is what I remember.

A dog and a crow.

Gilly called me on my cell phone as I was unpacking boxes in the kitchen of our new rental.

"We're here in the front yard, but can't get out of the truck. There's a dog growling at us," Gilly said as I walked toward the window facing the front yard. A blackish-brown dog that looked part pit bull, part snarling monster, ears bowed back, was standing rigidly by the driver's side of the flatbed truck that Gilly and her friend were in. As our menacing new neighbor let out a guttural bark, showing his teeth, Mike pulled up in his car and blared his horn to chase off the animal.

Stan, another neighbor, had called the police when the dog wouldn't leave his yard earlier the same day, saying the dog was a constant danger, pinning homeowners in their cars, garages, backyards. Later, Stan and Mike approached the dog's owner, our next door neighbor, hoping to address the Cujo situation in a non-threatening neighborly way.

"That didn't go well," Mike said as he came in from the garage, his brows furrowed. "I think she thought I was the one who called the cops. She told me to mind my own Goddamned business."

Then Gilly's friend joined us for a water break after moving a couch into the living room. We'd be able to sit on it and look out our front window facing the city park. I hadn't named a house since Oak Lane, but I thought this rental lent itself nicely to an official Mangan naming as an encouraging sign of permanence to Gilly, who was adjusting to Griffin's departure for college. She had lost her brother as her steady companion for sixteen years and the tri-level bedroom that she loved in the same month. Silly fun, naming a structure.

"What do you think about calling this house 'Park View?'" I asked Gilly and her friend as we chugged down iced-cold water.

"More like 'Drug View,'" Gilly's friend quipped.

"What?" Gilly and I both asked.

"The park is known for drug deals," he said sheepishly. "But maybe the police have gotten it under control."

"Well, I think this is going to be a great new home for making new memories and traditions," I said optimistically, trying to assure Gilly and myself. Hope had remained the one constant wherever we lived and I was determined it would follow us here, to our home by the park.

·   ·   ·   ·   ·   ·

Two days before the Fourth of July, Gilly was to wake up early to begin her daily seven a.m. summer varsity volleyball practice. The night before, however, she wasn't sure if she'd go. The past few days had been an exhausting pace of moving out of the tri-level into the new house. Maybe she'd sleep in, she said. Fine by me, I told her.

My alarm went off at six-fifteen. Sleepily, I put on my white robe and headed toward the front door to let out Honey and get the newspaper. I heard Gilly moving about in her bedroom. I guess she's going to practice, I thought. Picking up the paper from the driveway, a nasal, high-pitched cawing noise came from the morning sky. Looking up, I saw a group of black crows circling above me. And right over Honey. They began cawing in unison, loudly.

"C'mon, Honey, let's go inside," I said shooing the dog up the front steps.

When I got inside, I went into the hallway near Gilly's room, where I'd stored some of her volleyball knee pads in the hall closet.

"I'm getting your knee pads!" I yelled to Gilly.

As I went to grab a box on the closet's top shelf, I heard what sounded like a loud thud. Gilly must have dropped something, I thought.

"You okay?" I yelled.

"Gilly?"

Walking into her room, the light was on in her bathroom.

"Gilly?"

As I reached her bathroom, I saw her arm on the pink-tiled bathroom floor.

Twitching. Rounding the corner, I found Gilly sprawled by the toilet, violently contracting on the floor, contorting and flexing, biting her lip, unconscious.

Instinctively, I turned her on her side and screamed for Mike who was still asleep in our bedroom.

"Mike! Mike! Mike!" I screamed again, praying Mike would hear me. He was deaf in his right ear, a result of a viral infection a few years earlier, and our room was on the other side of the house. I couldn't leave Gilly.

"Mike!"

Please, God, let him hear me.

Mike ran into Gilly's bedroom.

"Call 9-1-1!" I yelled while I held Gilly's head to her side to stop her from hitting her temple on the bathroom cabinet. An egg-sized red knot was forming on the right side of her forehead.

"Wake up, baby. Please wake up," I cried.

I remember Mike standing over Gilly and me, staying on the phone with the 9-1-1 operator until the ambulance arrived. The EMTs, two young men, wheeled a stretcher into Gilly's room. Gilly began to breathe heavily, moaning, slowly opening her eyes after what felt like an hour, but had been only a few minutes. She was confused. Her swollen tongue trickled blood down her chin as they wheeled her outside, still not knowing where she was.

"Post-ictal," one of the EMTs said. "Typical for a grand mal."

I remember running into my closet to put on a pair of sweatpants and a shirt...and the splattered drops of red on my robe as I threw it on the carpet. I ran back to the ambulance to ride with Gilly, now conscious and crying, looking down at the I.V. in her hand. Mike would follow us in his car to the hospital. I was shaking so hard I couldn't stop, my hands trembling as I held onto the side of the ambulance to step inside. I didn't want Gilly to notice so I sat on my hands on the cold metal bench as the blue uniformed man with a crew cut closed the ambulance doors. As we drove away, I remember looking out the back window to make sure Mike was behind us. I saw two large black crows perched on the flag painted with a "Welcome" greeting which I had hung on the front yard's pine tree the week before.

·   ·   ·   ·   ·   ·

Six weeks.

That's what we aim for, Gilly's neurologist said in our follow-up visit, referencing our objective to keep her seizure-free for six weeks. It's an encouraging sign if we can get that distance between her and her grand mal, he added. Six weeks would be the first day of Gilly's high school junior year and the busiest time of the year for her on her state champion volleyball team after the fall season began. Two-a-day practices would not be part of her healing regime, breaking Gilly's heart even though her coach and teammates assured her she'd be on the team no matter what. Plus, the junior year in the International Baccalaureate Honors High School was known to be the most academically rigorous, although Gilly had sailed through her first two years just fine.

And absolutely no driving. Florida law prohibited driving for six months after having a seizure.

"That's okay, mama, I can stay busy working on my summer assignments to get ready for the school year," Gilly said as we returned home from her doctor's appointment, intent on proving to Mike and me, and to herself, this set-back wasn't going to bring her down.

Awe-struck by Gilly's resilience, I was determined to be like my sixteen-year-old daughter. This would not define us. We would beat this.

Gilly's blood work indicated her anti-seizure medicine was too low to be effective, meaning Mike and I had unintentionally under-dosed her. The directions on the bottle had called for five hundred milligrams of Zarontin twice a day. Amidst the chaos of packing and moving for the past month, Mike and I had incorrectly given Gilly her medicine once a day, half of what was prescribed. That, plus being tired from the move and waking up too quickly on that morning, was the perfect storm for a grand mal.

So, Gilly kept herself busy, but at a good pace for someone whose brain needed to heal. She entertained friends and teammates who visited, tried to learn to knit with her Aunt JuJu—while they sat on the couch laughing as a ball of yarn rolled across the floor—read Jane Austen, stayed hydrated, took the right dosage of medicine two times a day, and got a good eight to ten hours of sleep, usually heading to bed no later than ten p.m. and waking by eight a.m at the latest.

"One day at a time, mama," my sweet Gilly Girl would say.

As Gilly diligently worked to heal and reach her summer six-week seizure-free goal, Mike and I struggled to overcome our mutual guilt. Gilly trusted us to care for her, to make sure she was taking the right dosage of her epilepsy medicine. To stay rested. Always a mindful daughter, Gilly did exactly what we asked of her when it came to staying healthy. And what did we do in return?

"We screwed up," I said to Mike as we carried Gilly's trundle bed spare mattress into our bedroom where she would sleep beside us in case she had another seizure. "We were so damn busy moving that we didn't pay attention to the dosage of her meds. And if she was getting enough sleep."

"I know. But we can't go back. Let's just focus on getting her healthy," Mike said as he tucked a mattress sheet around the corners of Gilly's bed.

Which is exactly what we did. We all got into a better pattern of "Circadian sleep" as Gilly's doctor had prescribed. Our diet was healthier. We eliminated most sugars and empty carbs from our meals. A few weeks after her grand mal, Gilly began to take slow-and-easy walks with me around the park.

The week before school started, Gilly sat next to me on the couch before dinner. Her countenance was uncharacteristically subdued even though my sixteen-year-old daughter was about to reach her six-week goal of no seizures.

"I'm not sure I want to go back to I.B.," Gilly said, her lower lip quivering. "I love school and my volleyball team and my friends, but I don't want to risk having another seizure."

Gilly verbalized what I had been thinking. Her accelerated classes plus volleyball games at night would not be an ideal formula for a healing epileptic. But, I believed Gilly could manage it if that's what she wanted. As a parent, I discovered more about my children's character during times of stress than during times of ease. Gilly showed me resilience personified as she dealt with her health condition. Self-pity wasn't in her DNA. Self-driven was.

Determined to remain focused on what she could accomplish, instead of what she couldn't, Gilly stayed current with her summer assignments. She was diligent about her recovery regimen and set her cell phone alerts to make sure she took her medicine on time, drank enough water, and slept adequately. Getting better was her sole mission.

The I.B. school was across town. The public high school she was zoned for, which Griffin had graduated from, was literally across the street from my office. I could be there in five minutes, two if the traffic light was green.

Which is how we found ourselves sitting in the Forest High School guidance counselor's office three days before school started, signing Gilly up for advanced placement classes.

"Hey, look at this," the counselor said as she clicked on her computer to finalize Gilly's transfer from I.B. to Forest, "You're number one in your junior class here."

As we walked into the school lobby, Gilly asked Mike what he thought about her trying out for the Forest High varsity volleyball team, a good group of girls with a less stressful workout schedule than her previous team. Mike dialed the head coach on his cell phone. Hanging up, he smiled.

"Coach said practice is tonight and he'd love for you to come," Mike said as we stood in the lobby, all absorbing what just happened. "What do you think, Gilly?"

Gilly looked at us both and then gave a megawatt smile, the first I'd seen since July.

"YOLO!" Gilly said, laughing.

You Only Live Once.

And for every practice, every game, either Mike or I stayed with Gilly—usually it was Mike—offering bottled water, Gatorade and encouragement. Unspoken anxiety was present during the first few practices, more for Mike and me than for our ever-hopeful and determined daughter as she beamed, running around the court in her new team jersey.

Mike and I worried, what if she collapsed? What if she had a seizure while practicing? Yet, her coach and teammates surrounded Gilly with a determination to keep her safe and healthy as much as she did herself. If she felt tired, a teammate would sit out a practice rotation and gulp Gatorade and share a few teenage-girl giggles on the bench. And for that, I loved every single one of them. High school females can be a breed of pettiness and narcissism, but I saw none of that during Gilly's season of healing. The same giving spirit was shared in the classroom, too. Her new teachers and new friends welcomed Gilly with open arms and hearts, making her transition as easy and positive as possible, gestures of love none of us would ever forget.

In September, the first time her new volleyball team played against her old team, her former teammates ran across the gym, picked up Gilly and carried her around like a baby, her legs wrapped tightly around the six-foot outside hitter's waist as friends, teachers and the principal lined up to see her.

I once read a quote that said, "When one door closes, another one opens. Or you can open the closed door. That's how doors work." Gilly reminded me time and again that she was not one to walk away from a closed door. She'd pick the lock open if she had to. She didn't give up her passion for volleyball. She pushed herself just enough to maintain her self-imposed high academic standards. She invited more friends, not less, into her circle of Gillyness, refusing to let a closed door keep her from living the life she wanted, albeit with a few modifications.

By April, I realized I had gotten the hang of this partial empty nest routine with Griffin ebbing in and out of our home on college breaks. I could go five weeks without laying eyes on my boy. That was my limit. Any longer would leave me restless. I still missed him more than I thought possible, especially after Gilly's grand mal. It was during this time that I realized how our family unit had become a unified fortress, best shielding us from harm when we were all together. Griffin had a way of calming all of us, especially his little sister, who missed him terribly, so we adapted. Texting became a welcome link. Every night before bedtime, Griffin and I would touch base the new-fashioned way, by cell phone.

HOPE YOU HAD A GOOD DAY AT SCHOOL. HEADING TO BED. I SURE LOVE YOU.

I DID! HOPE YOU DID, TOO. I LOVE YOU MORE.

IMPOSSIBLE.

NOT IMPOSSIBLE.

Seldom did I take for granted that my nineteen-year-old son kept me included in his new and exciting world of college. It was a new dance neither of us had performed before, but we both did our best to fall into a routine where we didn't step on each other's toes. And there was no greater joy then when Griffin would call me. Complete bliss! Nothing better than seeing Griffin's name on my caller ID.

"Hey, sweet son!"

"Hi, Mom. How are you?"

"I'm good. How are you?"

"I'm doing well," Griffin said. "My international affairs professor is really cool. Did you know that Tallahassee has a high percentage of human trafficking? He's hosting a forum about this next week that I'm going to."

I'd often told my children that my college years were some of the happiest times. I relished being in an intellectually stimulating and challenging environment. By all accounts, Griffin did as well—solace for missing him so.

That, plus keeping Gilly healthy, helped buffer the physical space between my firstborn and me.

Seizure-free weeks turned into months and, before I knew it, summer arrived, close to Gilly's one-year seizure mark while also bringing Griffin home. He worked at a glass manufacturing plant to earn his own "walking around money" as my dad used to say.

July meant we'd made it.

A year since Griffin left home for college. A year without a seizure for Gilly. A year of managing medicine and rest and work schedules and high school classes. Mike and I assumed the tasks we were best suited for. Me, the organizer and communicator, creating a three-inch thick notebook of EEG tests, blood work, typed notes from every doctor's visit. Syncing my phone alarm with Gilly's for her twice-a-day meds. Mike was her daily chauffeur, driving her to and from school, volleyball practice and games, always staying close by when she was working out with her team. He made sure she ate well, always cutting up fresh apples, strawberries and pineapples for her snacks. He washed sweaty spandex and gym socks and workout clothes while Gilly studied after practice. While limited in opportunity, Mike's job afforded him a flexible work schedule. I honestly don't know what we would have done if both of us had the same work expectations. Traveling was easier for me knowing Mike was caring for Gilly.

This was the year Mike and I learned about the intrinsic value of being a caregiving couple. We were good at it, swapping responsibilities when we needed to and helping each other out when the other needed a break. It sure as hell wasn't the role we wanted to assume, but we were glad we were able to. I parked the idea of divorce in the back lot of my mind. Mike and I were stronger, unified to protect our daughter. It was a year of healing for us, too.

But it also meant the end of our lease option for our rental. No way could we buy the house on the park. Luckily, our landlord was the mother of a wonderful high school friend who graciously agreed to let us rent for one more year before having to make a purchase decision. They could have easily put the house on the market. Real estate was picking up again, but they liked us living in their Ocala home. The mom and her son lived in Texas and this was the house they had grown up in. The sentimental attachment for them was as deep as their late father's carved initials in the wall of his woodworking office that I now used as my writing space. We were given a respite.

"You know what's coming up soon, don't you?" Mike asked as Griffin and Gilly set the table for our Fourth of July baby back ribs dinner.

"Dessert?" I asked joking.

"Your birthday!" the kids answered in unison.

"It's your fiftieth. We need to do something," Mike said as he poured an Arnold Palmer lemonade-tea into our glasses.

"Let's have a party!" Gilly, my natural party planner, said.

I had never had a birthday party, at least not a big one with invited guests and cake and frivolity. My preferred celebrations were smaller scale, more intimate, usually with our movie club, a group of two other couples Mike and I saw movies with once a month followed by dinner. In the past five years, these friends had become practically the only group we would go out with. They knew our story and loved us through it. If we couldn't afford dinner out, one of the couples would make a meal at their place. I felt safe with them without feeling the need to explain the latest crisis.

"Let's just have dinner with the movie club," I said to Mike, handing him a bowl of coleslaw.

Mike leaned in, pulling me toward him.

"The kids and I want to celebrate Mama with a party here," he said and tenderly kissed me on my temple.

"That's okay," I said changing the subject.

After dinner and watching neighbors launch fireworks from the park, I returned the ice cooler to the closet next to our dining room. One thing about this house, it had ample storage, eight closets for a four-bedroom home. As a result, we filled up each closet with stuff. Board games, totes of files, a portable card table and four chairs that friends gave to us after they had moved out of town, suitcases, the mirrored-headboard to our dresser that didn't fit in our master bedroom, winter jackets, beach towels.

I remembered when we had none of these things. When we had downsized to an apartment of essentials only. Consumption had slowly crept back into our lives, yet what did we have to show for it? We could afford board games and totes from Walmart, but not a mortgage. Nor, most especially, living in a house that I wanted, like the ones online I'd scan every night on my laptop as I drifted asleep dreaming of the cute three bedroom, two bath just listed on Zillow.

Nope. No birthday party for me at the Drug View house. If I were honest, I felt ashamed of where I lived. And ashamed to be ashamed. We were damn lucky to be in the house. The rental was well-built and well-loved by its owners, but it wasn't mine. It wasn't my choice. And the dog and the crows, well, there was that. Too much bad karma already. Consequently, I seldom invited friends over. They'd have to drive around the sparsely landscaped city park and by Cujo's home with the overgrown lawn and the car without tires left on the driveway.

And they'd see my small box of a kitchen of dark brown cabinets, lit with inefficient lighting so dim I used a flashlight to read recipes. The linoleum floor in the former game room was peeling at the corners. Guests would trip if they came over. And the air conditioning whirred like a jet engine drowning out any decent conversation.

All excuses. A feeble cover-up to keep my secret securely stored away like the items in my house of many closets.

But the jig was up, wasn't it? People knew. How could they not? And why did I still care? Gilly's grand mal had stripped away the veneer of giving a damn about what other people thought. It simply didn't matter. So, why the reluctance to let people into our house?

Because we were broke.

Still living paycheck to paycheck.

Climbing out of debt was more like clawing up a sand dune. We never got over the top. And we were careful about every penny. We had to be. But, it was still Every. Damn. Penny. That's what this house represented to me. The stigma of having nothing to show for the struggle. It was all I could see in the crown molding, the jalousie windows, the medieval light fixture that blinked erratically in the guest bathroom. Our permanent weakness, our failure to ever make it right laced with the impervious shame of seemingly never knowing how to. By the time I was fifty, I was certain I'd have a place of my own and a bank account to match. A nest and a nest egg.

"Mama, let's have a dance party," Gilly said, interrupting my thoughts as she stood outside of the walk-in closet.

"Dada, Griffin and I will plan it," she said. "Remember how we used to dance at Oak Lane?"

"Yes, I remember."

"There's no reason we can't dance here," she said.

"I don't know," I said, shrugging my shoulders.

"Give me one good reason why not," Gilly said, putting both hands on my shoulder, locking her eyes with mine.

Right there, in that moment, staring at the brightest light right in front of me, I couldn't confess the shallowness of my shame. That's what I remember, the night I let it go. What the hell was I waiting for? Fifty years got here in warped speed.

I turned off the closet light and wrapped my arms around my daughter's neck.

"Okay," I said smiling. "YOLO!"

You only live once. It was time to dance again.

Chapter 17

The Game Room: The Rest of Forever

A few months before my fiftieth birthday, someone suggested I compile a "bucket list" to commemorate this milestone celebration that had earned me an AARP invitation and, apparently, a chance to list all the things I'd hope to do and see in this ripe old age that now afforded me restaurant discounts to use at early bird buffets. So I jotted down a few things on a piece of paper and placed it on my desk, since I've never known anyone who actually puts lists in a bucket.

This reminded me of the dream posters I had made ten years earlier with my friend to celebrate her fortieth birthday in my craft/laundry room at Oak Lane Cottage, painting our dreams and desires on canvases of "Why not?" But, after all I had been through since that time, I found myself asking, "Why bother at all?" I was hesitant to draft a list of rosy wishes for the next decade.

Still, I was a sucker for hope. And I had a dance party to prepare for. Fifty? Bring it on!

I decided to ascribe to a saying I'd once seen on a cocktail napkin, "Trust me. You can dance. Love, Vodka." Mike, Griffin, and Gillian formed a party committee with only a few requests from me, let there be music and martinis. And cake, especially the decadent chocolate and vanilla creation made by Bettycakes, my favorite Ocala bakery and café. And pink. I'm rather fond of the color pink. "Dancing & Dessert" invitations were mailed to friends and a disc jockey, whose business was called 'The Times of Your Life," was secured.

By the night of my party in early August, our rental had been turned into party central with pink crepe paper decorations, banners, rock candy, and a Bettycake. My friend Tracy and I created our own customized martini—a "Disco Ball-tini"—comprised of vodka, limoncello, grenadine and I don't remember what else because we added other ingredients to achieve that rare balance of sweet and alcohol-impactful. We also had virgin Disco Ball–tinis for my extended "children"—Griffin and Gilly's friends who had become like my own children through the years. Some of them were in college, the rest in high school. I loved that they wanted to come to Mama Mangz's party. And they were good dancers. That would loosen up the crowd.

The DJ held center court in our living room. Mike and Griffin had cleared it out for dancing. It adjoined my study, a spacious room facing the backyard which the home owners had previously used as a game room. As with most parties, guests ended up congregating in the study to take well-needed breaks from getting their boogie on nearby. Mama, now ninety, visited with guests as she sat on the couch and watched her baby girl perform a bad rendition of the Carolina Shag. Gilly made a dance party CD as favors for the guests. She included my favorites, "Best of My Love" by the Emotions, "Mr. Sunshine" by Electric Light Orchestra, "Fly Me to the Moon" by Frank Sinatra, "Beyond the Sea" by Bobby Darin, "September" by Earth, Wind and Fire. The party brought together my closest friends and family who all graciously cut the rug as I dragged them onto the dance floor beneath a mirrored ball splashing rainbow dots across their faces.

"Will you dance with your mama?" I asked Griffin. He gave me one of his big smiles as we laughed at our dance moves while bumping into my friend Tracy, who proved to be a far better shagger than the rest of us.

For the first time since we had left Oak Lane, I felt as light as the $9.99 Styrofoam disco ball spinning above me. It didn't matter one iota that my house was a rental with a cramped kitchen, peeling flooring, and a neighbor who raised attack dogs for sport. I was with those whom I loved the most and that alone was a reason to dance.

•   •   •   •   •   •

Seven weeks later I hosted another party, this time a wedding shower for my niece Lisa and her fiancé, Matt. Griffin wanted to drive down from Tallahassee. It had been five weeks since he left Ocala to begin his sophomore year at F.S.U. We were planning to visit with him the following week so I told him not to worry about coming to the shower. He had a full load of challenging classes and a new part-time job with a state agency. I wanted to see him, but didn't want him tired from a quick trip to Ocala. Saying it might be the last time he would see Lisa and Matt before they moved to California, though, he decided to arrive on Friday night after work.

If Griffin had chosen not to make the trip to Ocala that weekend, I now believe I might never have seen my son alive again.

Just before the sun set on a September Friday, Griffin pulled into the driveway. Mike, Gilly and I rushed out to the car to hug him as he unloaded his suitcase and guitar. When he came around the car, I was taken aback by his appearance. Griffin, dressed in a university garnet-colored shirt and khaki shorts, was visibly gaunt, his shorts hanging on his thin frame. I didn't want to alarm him or sound like a nagging mother the first minute we were together, so I refrained from asking about his weight.

"Take a picture, mama," Gilly said, dressed in her high school volleyball uniform. She always wanted a photo with her big brother when he came home.

Clicking my cell phone camera as Gilly hugged Grif, I felt a heaviness of worry and fear in my chest. It didn't go away the next day during the wedding shower or the early evening when we went to one of Griffin's favorite Thai restaurants for dinner where he picked at his Chicken Pad Thai and left a plate of uneaten noodles. We returned home and watched a little television while visiting before everyone went to bed. Grif came into our master bedroom to hug us goodnight. I casually asked him to weigh himself on our scale in the bathroom. As he stood barefoot looking down, I read the numbers on the scale.

Twenty pounds.

Griffin had lost twenty pounds in five weeks.

I waited until Griffin went to bed to broach the subject of my concern with Mike.

"I think something is seriously wrong with Griffin," I said sitting on the bed. "He is way too thin and barely ate anything this weekend."

"He's a college student and probably doesn't have the best eating habits," Mike said. "Maybe we can talk to him before he heads back to Tallahassee tomorrow morning."

"I think we need to," I said. "But I'm afraid it's more than just not eating well."

On Sunday morning, Griffin joined Mike and me on the living room couch where we asked honest and open questions. Was he eating enough? How did he feel? Was there anything he needed to tell us?

Griffin shared our concern over his weight. Listening to my maternal gut, I told Griffin we needed to go to a health clinic before he headed back to

Tallahassee. Gilly was still asleep, so Mike and I offered one of us to go with him, the other to stay with her.

"If it's okay, I'd like you to go with me, mom," Griffin said.

Sitting in a patient's room in the clinic, Griffin and I talked about his classes and music and the *West Wing* until the nurse returned with results from Griffin's blood and urine tests. Her drawn face said it all.

"You are dropping sugar in your urine," the nurse said almost apologizing. "And your blood sugar is very high."

"Okay," Griffin said calmly. "What does that mean?"

"It means you are suffering from diabetic ketoacidosis," she said, "Oh, I'm so sorry, and you're so sweet. We need to get you to the hospital. I've already made a call for the emergency room to expect you."

There are moments in my life I'll always remember and Griffin's brave response was instantly engraved in my heart. Calmly, he listened as the nurse explained how diabetic ketoacidosis was the result of what happened when cells didn't get the glucose they need for energy, which produced ketones. When ketones had built up in the blood, they made it more acidic. If untreated, it could lead to coma or death.

Griffin politely nodded as the nurse described the cellular hell taking place inside him. He didn't fall apart. He didn't cry. He put on the best face he could to process what was happening, and his courage was both inspiring and God-awful heartbreaking.

I called Mike. I called our general physician, who called the hospital to alert them that Griffin would be there to be admitted shortly. I called my sisters and texted my friends. And then I drove Griffin to the emergency room.

"We will get you well, I promise you," I said holding Griffin's hand in the car.

"I know, mom. Maybe it's Type 2 diabetes, that's more manageable than Type 1," Griffin said, already researching his new diagnosis on his cell phone.

Within an hour of being admitted and with an IV of insulin flowing into his veins, Griffin was informed of his diagnosis. He had Type 1 Diabetes, a disease that doesn't run in our family, but neither did epilepsy. As the medical staff stabilized Griffin, Mike and I got a crash course in diabetes. For a diabetic, numbers are critical in blood sugar terms: 400 is bad, 120 is good. In the hospital, I kept a log of Griffin's blood sugar counts (as if the doctors weren't doing the same chartin—a parent will do anything to feel useful for her child.)

On one of my sleepless nights in the hospital, around three a.m., the nurse entered quietly into Griffin's room to prick his finger for the latest count. Grif's numbers had been high for the past few hours.

"Hey, look at that!" the nurse said, smiling. "You're at 120. Man, that's a rest-of-forever kind of number."

Indeed it was. A number Griffin could live with the rest of forever, if only it could be so. If only his blood sugar wouldn't spike up and down like a roller coaster with no end. I scribbled on my notepad in the dark. The next morning, I looked at my blood sugar count notes. Oddly, they were devoid of sugar counts. In a sleep-deprived fog, I had only written one thing. "Rest-of-forever."

Before this I had counted my life in different terms, in those things you'd see on a dream poster or a bucket list. Now I counted insulin units and EEG spikes for my mathematical formula of wishes. As our family adapted to Griffin's condition—not only on its own, but also in conjunction with his sister's epilepsy—I tried to keep it in perspective. I had friends who considered a good day measured by red blood cells. I'm certainly not the only person who has gone to bed as a wife, mother and daughter only to awake as a newly initiated (and scared) health care advocate for my loved ones. More than twenty-nine million Americans have diabetes. Almost three million have epilepsy. Millions more suffer from other life-threatening conditions.

They, and those who love them, assess their lives in ways not listed in glitter on a dream poster. So, in the Fall of 2014, I decided that this list thing might be backward. Life reminded me I should aspire more after who to be, not what to achieve. I had friends and family who showed up in emergency rooms on moving days and found resources to help in ways I didn't know existed. They made the speed bumps and ditches and everything in between bearable. And Griffin and Gillian showed grace and determination beyond their years. Beyond anything, really, I could've imagined facing for myself.

If I could be like them, my rest-of–forevers would trump all bucket lists and dream posters.

For a month after Griffin's diagnosis, Mike and I traded staying with him, first in Ocala and then when he had returned to his Tallahassee apartment. We slept on his bedroom floor, ready to hand him his blood sugar meter or a glucose tab when needed. We made sure he had ample supplies of juice boxes, bottles of glucose tabs, protein packs, needles for his injections, two kinds of daily insulin,

meter testing strips, meters, and an emergency Glucagon injection kit should he
become unconscious from an insulin low. I created an emergency call list of
Tallahassee friends who circled around Griffin as a protective tribe and reassured
Mike and me as we finally had to return home to Ocala, one of the hardest days of
my life.

It is a parent's wish to never see their children struggling with a life-altering
situation. I was no different. I wanted healthy and normal for Griffin and Gillian.
And when that ship of dreams had sailed, I compromised my approach. Let them
find peace and happiness in where they are, I prayed every night, every day, every
time I was at a stop sign.

Griffin's acceptance of the insidious and relentless condition that forced him
to be his own pancreas twenty-four hours a day was nothing short of jaw-
dropping inspiration. Amidst the finger pricking and insulin injections and blood
sugar highs and lows, Griffin never complained. Not once. He had the Mangan
stoicism which, I came to realize, served him well as a new diabetic. But, I ached
for him, knowing this was the time in his life he should feel the most independent
to explore the wonders of being a college-aged young man. Instead, he was
tethered to a continuous glucose monitoring system that alerted him when it was
time to inject or prick or drink a carb-rich juice.

"I'm really okay, mom," Griffin would say, more to reassure me than to focus
on himself.

"You're pretty amazing, you know that?" I said to Griffin as I sat on his bed in
his apartment.

"I don't know about that," he smiled, playing the new Radiohead song he
just learned.

I do, I thought, as I watched my son strum rich, throaty chords, lost in the
melody's haunting anthem.

"I sure love you," I said, finding my spot on his floor of my makeshift bed of
comforters, blankets and pillows.

"I love you more," Griffin said.

"Impossible," I said quietly as I closed my eyes.

"Not impossible," Griffin replied, carefully putting down his guitar and then
meter-checking his blood sugar before bedtime.

By end of October, Griffin had adapted well. He had already returned to
school and work, finding the regular patterns of college life to be a comforting

routine. We celebrated his twentieth birthday, truly acknowledging why birthdays are meant to be honored. It was my season of favorite birthdays as Gilly's was just around the corner.

At our next follow-up appointment with Griffin's endocrinologist at Shands Teaching Hospital in Gainesville, his doctor informed me Gilly would need to be tested to determine if she possessed the same genetic predisposition as Griffin to develop Type 1 diabetes. Her blood was drawn that day. I asked the nurse when we would get the results.

"November 14th" the nurse asked, raising her eyebrows. "Hey, that's the same date as World Diabetes Day."

It was also Gilly's eighteenth birthday. The same damn day.

This is when I had my come-to-Jesus talk with Jesus. Here's the deal, I said to the sky while driving back from Gainesville as Mike and Gilly drove in Mike's car in front of me. Enough is enough, I continued, talking aloud in my car. I get that I control very few things during my time on this earth and I've learned the lesson of letting things go and being in the now and focusing on what and who matters most. Bad things happen to good people and good things happen to bad people and I could go and on with this philosophical good and bad rant, but the driver in the next lane is looking at me, probably because I'm now sobbing uncontrollably and screaming into my windshield.

Are you listening to me, I yelled to God. No more. No. More. I know it's been said that we're never given more than we can handle, but I believe whoever said that was one of those rare good or bad people who never had bad things happen to them, or at least to their children. Therefore, they believe they can handle this. But, for me? Enough! Give *me* diabetes. Give *me* epilepsy. Do not let Gilly have diabetes, too, in addition to waking up every day scared she'll fall to the bathroom floor with a grand mal. And don't you dare think about Griffin having to face epilepsy. I really don't understand why this has happened to them, although I've chosen not to dwell on this subject because it doesn't change a damn thing and it doesn't help my children. I've taken my lumps for the Team of Life. I've been hungry, I've been penniless. I can deal with that. But I must ask you something, God, and I ask this with all the respect of a reformed Southern Baptist/Presbyterian/Brief Catholic. "What the hell are you thinking?"

My foot hit the brake pedal to distance myself from Mike and Gilly. They didn't need to see their hysterical wife and mother losing it. As we reached the Ocala city limits, I stopped crying. Forty-five miles of weeping was my limit, I decided, and I wiped my nose with a spare napkin from my glove compartment and pulled into a drive-thru to get a Diet Coke pick-me-up.

One week later, as Gilly blew out eighteen candles on her birthday cake, I received a text from Griffin's doctor. Gilly's test results showed she was not predisposed for Type 1 Diabetes. It was the best birthday gift she—or any of us—could have gotten.

Christmas gave me pause to reflect on another important gift—one that was a constant for our family—our network of support. Our holiday card acknowledged them. This year was all about appreciation for those who carried and cried and loved us through some very difficult days. A very close friend and talented photographer graciously took our family photo as we sat in the backyard on a cool November afternoon. Each year, I tried to capture the sense of family in a personalized verse:

"4:39 p.m. on a Friday

Close together, we pull in. The sun falls behind us as long shadows spread across the grass. Winter is approaching.

We have stood here before. Maybe not at this exact spot, but we've gathered in the same way to stop what we are doing for a moment and look into the lens. We are here. Closer, we smile."

I used the rest of the card's space to thank my friends and family for the food they brought, the prayers they offered, the medical connections we needed and the love that had filled our days of worry. Next to my words of gratitude, I included a photo with our best family pose, smiling officially for the camera, Honey included. The dog literally was a camera hound. She loved the lens. On the back of the card, I included what may very well remain on of my favorite pictures, Grif and Gilly cracking up in between photo takes, and another of Mike wrapping his arms around me as we both laughed hysterically.

We had been dealt with a crappy deck of cards of late, but we had each other and, for that, we found a reason to embrace joy.

·   ·   ·   ·   ·   ·

Just like Griffin's senior year in high school, Gilly's senior year flew right past me. And also just like Griffin, Gilly would leave home two weeks after high school graduation in June, but her first entrée into college wasn't on campus. It was in Mexico. Gilly received the University of Florida's Lombardi Scholars Honors Scholarship that earned her not only an academic scholarship into UF, but also international travel every summer with her other Lombardi scholars.

Earlier, during Gilly's junior year, she had begun a blog, "Finding Faces," using her love of writing and photography to draw attention to those facing epilepsy. She photographed other epileptics and shared their stories of how they successfully had navigated living their lives while managing their seizures.

"I was so scared when I was first diagnosed and didn't know anyone who had epilepsy," Gilly told me one night after showing me her newly created blog on our computer. "But now I know so many others who inspire me, so I want to help others by seeing the faces of success."

"Who is this kid and where did she come from?" I joked to Mike, sitting on the couch with me next to Gilly.

"I'm a Mangan!" Gilly said smiling.

Yes, she was.

A newspaper editor heard about Gilly's blog. Her husband was an epileptic. She wrote a story about Gilly and her blog which created such an outpouring of interest that Gilly's blog readers began averaging over five thousand hits per day.

"There are so many people wanting to share their story," Gilly said as she scrolled through her blog's comments section.

As Gilly packed for Mexico, I folded her shorts, Chacos, and too many Jane Austen paperback books into her carry-on suitcase.

"You know what July second is, don't you?" Gilly asked, handing me another pair of shorts to pack.

"Yes, I do," I nodded. Of course I knew. It would be two years since her grand mal. "Let's make sure we get to this date. Please be safe. Please be careful in Mexico."

"I will," Gilly said and rubbed my shoulder. "I promise."

•   •   •   •   •   •

When Gilly landed at Tampa International Airport six weeks later, our family had experienced more change. Grif stayed in Tallahassee that summer for the first time, working at his job and doing better with his diabetes. Gilly celebrated her two-year seizure free anniversary with a Mexican fiesta with her scholars group who had become instant good friends. Mike and I found ourselves as real empty nesters, returning home each night to each other and Honey, who had learned to embrace the concept of being the only "child" left home. And I returned to scratch my writing itch, accepting a freelance columnist gig for the local newspaper while also keeping my day job, which continued to push me in new and exciting ways.

My first column? My perspective on life since Gillian and Griffin's diagnoses. With an average of forty thousand readers, I hoped to convey the lessons I had learned thus far. And I was willing to share part of my story, too, how our financial struggles had often overshadowed everything else—until we discovered everything else suddenly mattered more. To my relief, my column was well-received. The editor sent me a lovely note of appreciation which still sits on my desk as a reminder to never stop writing again. And the readers' responses in e-mails and calls and texts reminded me that life's challenges can be universal.

My fifty-first birthday rolled around in early August. Mike and I discovered there was a salsa night at a local restaurant. Mike, Gilly and some friends joined me for a night of dining and dancing. Griffin had come home the weekend before for an early birthday celebration. After enjoying mojitos and Cuban sandwiches, we watched dancers of all ages and abilities come together for this electric and joyful dance. Mike pulled me onto the floor. Gilly joined us. We swayed back and forth. I laughed at our amateur salsa moves and gleefully let myself get lost in song.

"Let's get a picture of us!" Gilly yelled over the booming base of the music.

Mike snapped a photo of mother and daughter hugging in front of the crowded dance floor. Gilly's long blond hair framed her face as she hugged her fifty-one-year-old salsa-loving mother.

The next week, we moved Gilly into her dorm in Gainesville in mid-August. My baby had left home. A year before, she was making dance party CDs for my fiftieth birthday party. A year before, Griffin had tied pink balloons to our mailbox to welcome guests to the Mangan Disco Club. A year before, Mike and I didn't know what September would bring us or would bring Griffin.

"Remember to get rest and stay hydrated and never walk alone and always have your cell phone and don't stay out late," I said to Gilly, rattling off my maternal admonitions and hoping I hadn't forgotten anything. "And don't accept an open container drink from anyone. And make sure someone walks with you to and from your night class. Remember your cousin Holly lives close by and can be here in five minutes and I can be up here in forty-five minutes if you need me."

Gilly gave a big grin and hugged me once more.

"I know, mama," she said, squeezing me a little tighter. "I will be very careful. I love you."

"I love you more," I said as my entire internal organs started moving up through my throat.

"That's impossible," Gilly whispered in my ear, still locked in our embrace.

I just shook my head, unable to respond, trying to keep my emotions from spilling out.

As we drove away from Gilly's dorm, I thought of the times of my life that had given me the most joy. And those were divided into a distinct before and after category. Before children, and after. There was so much wonderful after. Even in the dark moments that greatly impacted both Griffin and Gillian's lives. They gave me joy. Hope. Inspiration. And now my baby girl was about to chart her own path. Just as Griffin had. Just as Mike and I would learn to do.

Let this next year be a good one, I prayed in the car to the heavens above, looking through the windshield on a sunny, cloudless August day. Then Mike turned onto the highway and I lost my rear view of Gilly standing outside her dorm waving goodbye.

Chapter 18

The Dining Room: Fall Risk

Seven years after our lives fell apart, Mike and I finally both had secure jobs that gave us some financial breathing room. He was five months into working as a large account manager for the same utility company where I worked, where I'd received a five-year work anniversary crystal plaque the week before. Griffin was enjoying his junior year at F.S.U. and part-time job helping adults who were former foster children gain employability skills. And Gilly was embracing life as a Florida Gator, pledging a sorority and finding her academic bliss as an English major.

What a difference a year makes, I thought one night, as Mike and I indulged in takeout pasta fagioli and chicken parmesan from our favorite restaurant. I even lit the usually neglected candle in the middle of our expansive dining table that weighed significantly more even than its matching six chairs. They had once belonged to Mike's grandmother and were ornately designed and solid mahogany antiques that each weighed the size of a small child and were an indulgent remnant spared from our moves.

My cell phone buzzed as I was mid-bite. When I saw Gilly's name on the caller ID, I answered and listened as she told me she'd had a good day. She raved about her cool poetry professor and how Taylor, her roommate, was so nice. "And the walk from my dorm to my classes isn't that long," she said excitedly. "Oh, and I'm staying on top of my homework. I'll send you a poem I wrote for class."

"That sounds wonderful, baby," I said, smiling at Mike, who was waiting for his turn to say hi. "Are you getting enough sleep?"

"Yes, ma'am. I'm in bed by ten thirty every night, Mama," Gilly replied. "And Taylor is so sweet, making sure I get the rest I need."

"Good. Say, what's on your schedule for tomorrow?" I asked.

"I have my morning classes and..." Gilly began to say.

Then it happened.

"Ahhhhhhh!" Gilly let out a loud, piercing moan, like a frightened, wounded animal trying to find shelter from the pain. The screeching howl was so profound, it stunned me for a second.

The phone went silent.

"Gilly! Gilly!" I screamed into the phone.

Nothing.

I yelled her name again. I don't know why I did, but I handed the phone to Mike as if he could make her answer.

"Gilly! Honey! Are you okay?" he asked urgently, though characteristically calmly, as I quickly pulled away from the table, sending my chair crashing onto the brick floor. Mike kept yelling her name into the phone, but I knew what had happened.

Somewhere in a city an hour away my daughter was having a grand mal seizure. I did not know where she was or who was with her, if anyone. All I knew was that the darkness had returned and had evicted us out of our temporary sanctuary.

Because Gilly had managed her epilepsy for the past two years without any episodes, her neurologist was considering weaning her off her medication, yet we agreed to wait until winter. She was almost home free. Perfect timing to begin college, we said.

Then, one month earlier and almost one year to the day since Griffin's diabetes diagnosis, she had had an unexpected grand mal while napping in her dorm.

Her doctor attributed it to the stress of adjusting to college and living away from home, an anomaly after doing so well for so long. Gilly just needed rest and new anti-seizure medicine to be safe, he said reassuringly. She spent the weekend with us recalibrating. Reluctantly, I let her return to UF where she worked hard to be an atypical college student getting plenty of rest and avoiding stress and alcohol (an absolute no for an epileptic). Things would soon return to normal.

But nothing had been normal in our lives. Why would we have thought this would be different? And yet, we did. Mike and I clinked our water glasses in a toast to the seemingly welcome ordinary after we had sat down for dinner.

Before we could begin our nicely quiet meal, Gilly called to tell us about her very good day.

Then Mike clenched the phone and began calling out Gilly's name over and over.

"Gilly, Gilly. It's okay, sweetie, if you can hear us, we are coming to you," he said. His voice was cracking as he gently cried into the vacant space between him and our daughter convulsing on the floor of God knows where.

I ran into the bedroom intending to grab my shoes from my closet and pack an overnight bag, a maternal reflex anticipating a night in the emergency room. Mike and I would drive to Gainesville and find her. We would call 9-1-1. Yes, that is what we would do. They could track Gilly by her phone, right? Was she walking on campus or in her dorm? Maybe she was in the university library's Special Collections room, her favorite place. Why didn't I ask her when she called?

Where was she?

I tried not to imagine my sweet, vivacious daughter alone and unconscious, just as I had learned not to fixate on the thought of Griffin, three hours away from me, falling into permanent sleep from an insulin high or low. Just as I learned not to obsess about where I'd live next or how I'd pay rent or what the road ahead had in store for me. I had learned how to cope and keep the demons at bay. I knew what to pack and what to let go.

I couldn't find my shoes or my tote. I was mistakenly in my bathroom. I looked into the mirror and saw a fragile, shaking woman who couldn't remember where the closet was. There had been so many closets. So many rooms. The woman in the mirror started spinning and I heaved into the sink as Italian red sauce burned my throat. I held onto the bathroom counter to steady myself. I had to get a grip. Gilly needed me.

Grabbing Mike's phone, I called Gilly's roommate.

"Taylor, Gilly is having a seizure. Do you know where she is?"

"Oh, no! Yes, ma'am, I just left her in our dorm room. I'm at my sorority house," she said, breathing into the phone already starting a fast sprint. "I'll run back right now!"

"I've called 9-1-1. Make sure she is on her side, not choking. We are heading to Gainesville right now. We will meet you at the emergency room," I said as I ran into my closet and slipped on my worn leather flats. Then I did what I knew how to do best.

I packed my bag and got moving.

·   ·   ·   ·   ·   ·

Five seizures. Three emergency room visits. Four calls to 9-1-1, one in our car on the rural highway a half hour outside of Tallahassee after we celebrated Griffin's twenty-first birthday in October. From September through November, Gilly's seizures could not be controlled, no matter how many new drugs she was taking. Her EEG and MRI tests did not reveal any new medical development other than the fact her condition had "evolved" as her doctor said, now concerned we were dealing with a different kind of epilepsy, maybe even more than one. He wanted to admit Gilly to Shands Teaching Hospital's Epilepsy Video Unit (EVU) where she would be withdrawn from her medicines and undergo an elevated EEG and hyperventilation test to induce a seizure where her brain activity could be monitored and recorded to—hopefully—accurately identify the origin of her seizures.

"The right diagnosis will give us the right medical treatment," he said to me on the phone the week before Thanksgiving.

I could not fathom Gilly being induced into having another grand mal, but I couldn't imagine sustaining what she was going through much longer. On the first day of December, Gilly was admitted to what the nurses on the hospital floor called "The Epilepsy Torture Unit."

Grabbing her school backpack and pink floral tote packed with her laptop, books, pajamas, favorite blankets and stuffed animals, Gilly stepped out of the car at the hospital entrance.

"Let's do this," she said, smiling to Mike and me with the grace and grit of a wise old woman in a nineteen-year-old body.

Once she was admitted, a nurse securely placed on Gilly's wrist a bright yellow plastic bracelet with the words "FALL RISK."

•   •   •   •   •   •

Waiting for a seizure to occur is like waiting for the boogie man in a horror flick to jump from behind the door. You know it's going to happen, you just don't know when. And so we waited. Gilly's bandaged head concealed electrodes that were connected to a wire connected to an EEG monitoring system in the wall. Bathroom trips were tricky, requiring both of us to hold the wires and cords as Gilly carefully walked a few steps from her hospital bed to the bathroom.

Privacy was another challenge, as in there was none. Gilly was being watched twenty-four hours a day by EEG monitoring staff in another room connected by a camera installed near the ceiling. Daily the nurses would change Gilly's electrodes while they'd stand over her head like hair stylists and call out numbers to the camera in the ceiling. A voice would project from a nearby speaker, like Oz, informing the nurse of a loose electrode connection.

Sometimes we'd forget about our ever-present observers. Propped up in her bed, Gilly showed me a funny video on her laptop of a guy dressed in a little frock and acting like a housewife frantically cleaning before guests arrived.

"These pillows need to be FLUFFED!" he said running around in circles punching couch pillows.

The big event each day was morning rounds when doctors followed by interns followed by nurses came to see Gilly. They would arrive any time between seven and ten in the morning, three hours of worrisome anticipation for patients and families desperate to receive the latest medical update. The second morning in the EVU, I peeked into the hallway for signs of doctor life. It was almost ten a.m. and we were anxious to know what the plans were for the day, especially since Gilly was now off all her meds.

"Hey, they're in the next patient's room," I said to Gilly.

"The guests are coming!" Gilly said, giving a big grin from her bed.

"These pillows need to be FLUFFED!" I said grabbing the pillow from my couch bed, running in circles laughing with my Gilly Girl who, once again, reminded me of her fearless optimism and spirit.

That's when I realized I, too, was being recorded.

"Well, at least we're giving the monitoring team some comic relief," I said and returned my small pillow back to the couch.

When the group of doctors and nurses arrived to Gilly's room, they advised us they were upping the ante on seizure inducement by ordering exercise equipment and an evening EEG test. Just in time for Mike to arrive from his out-of-town work trip, I thought to myself, grateful I would not be alone for another night. Family members are asked to be seizure observers, too, so I slept lightly the night before, jumping up each time Gilly would move or stretch or yawn, fearing a grand mal. I was instructed to immediately push the emergency call button if Gilly began to seize. Sometimes lowering or eliminating medications could lead to a bigger seizure that lasts longer than normal. Doctors and nurses would need to give medicine to act quickly to stop it if it occurred during testing.

"All we really need is a recording of the first thirty seconds to pinpoint the seizure's origin," Gilly's doctor said. He visited the EVU, staying for over an hour every single night Gilly was hospitalized even though he wasn't on call that week.

Keeping Gilly focused on anything besides an impending seizure was my priority, but the best preoccupation was her friends who came to visit—her fellow university scholars who had traveled with her to Mexico, her Ivy House dorm buddies, her Zeta sorority sisters—piling into her small hospital bed looking at videos and pictures on their phones, talking about their final exams coming up. Aunt Julie and Aunt Cindy visited, too, and shared puppy and cousin stories with Gilly. Out of town friends had flowers, cookies and a stuffed teddy bear delivered.

Mike arrived at eight o'clock that night while Gilly was visiting with Patrick, a Lombardi scholar who was a youth volunteer staff member on the hospital floor. Patrick was starting medical school at UF. He too suffered from a chronic condition, debilitating rheumatoid arthritis at the ripe old age of twenty-one. He said his condition inspired him to go into the medical field and work in his current job at Shands helping youth and college-aged young adults who have to be hospitalized.

Doctors' orders were to keep Gilly awake all night until she seized. A nurse wheeled in an exercise bike.

"Seriously?" I asked the nurse.

"It may be part of the test if we can't induce a seizure from the EEG," the nurse said, nodding her head, giving me a "sometimes-I-hate-this-job" look. She was Leslie. And she was young and funny and instantly connected with Gilly, taking breaks from her rounds to visit with Gilly and watch videos with her.

Mike put his overnight bag on the rocking chair next to Gilly's bed.

"Hey, baby," he said, hugging Gilly as Patrick and Leslie moved the bike closer to the wall. "This is a busy place."

Patrick excused himself to go on a mission to find Gilly's favorite movies to watch together with her in her room.

"I'll be right back," Patrick said. "We can have a movie night marathon."

He's done this before, I thought, helping epileptic patients in the EVU as they wait for the beast to arrive.

An EEG technologist wheeled in monitoring equipment with a strobe light. He began talking to the voice coming from the ceiling speaker.

"Are we ready to start?" he asked looking up.

"We're ready," a male voice responded from a speaker above us.

"Wait, are you doing an EEG right now?" I asked, concerned that it was just Mike, me and this EEG man I didn't know there in the room with Gilly. "Don't we need a doctor and nurse here, too?"

"No, it's fine," he said matter-of-factly, "You need to stand by her and push this button if she seizes."

A hundred things were going in my mind, but one of them was that Gilly would not seize from an EEG test. She never had before. And she had only been off her medicine since that morning. I held Gilly's arm as the tech began the first part of the test. Mike stood beside me.

"You've done this before," I said, smiling to Gilly to reassure her although she was the one reassuring me.

"I know, Mama," Gilly said, staring straight into my eyes.

The nurse turned off the lights, leaving only the wall light on behind Gilly's bed. He started asking Gilly to breathe in and out quickly, forcing mild hyperventilation.

"I want you to breathe in and breathe out quickly until I tell you to stop," the nurse said as he stood over his mobile EEG machine.

Gilly inhaled. And exhaled. And inhaled. And exhaled for what seemed like a longer period of time than normally.

"Stop," the voice from the wall said. The nurse looked up. I looked at Gilly, who looked mildly distressed, but anyone would be after a prolonged hyperventilation exam. I held tight to her arm.

"Okay, go on," the voice ordered.

The nurse turned on the strobe light and asked Gilly to close her eyes. Flick. Flick. Flick. The light shone directly into Gilly's closed eyes. I looked away toward Mike, away from the jarring strobe flashing, moving my arm from Gilly's. Just as I did, I felt it. The beast. It had come.

Gilly raised her head, opening her mouth as if to yawn, showing her teeth, and then letting out a loud scream. Her vocal chords were seizing, forcing air out. As she howled, she raised her knees and her body started to convulse, shaking her from side to side. Her arms and legs stiffened as tremors consumed her from head to toe.

"Stop! Stop!" the voice from the wall commanded as the nurse turned off the strobe light and rushed to turn on all the lights. I pushed the emergency button again and again, yelling for help, hoping the voice in the wall was calling for help, too. Two doctors and several nurses, including Leslie, rushed in and surrounded Gilly, now in full grand mal seizure. It was lasting longer than ever before and was more violent as she jerked from side to side, shaking, biting her tongue.

"Help her!" I cried and held Gilly's head to her side toward me as one doctor checked her breathing. Leslie was leaning toward Gilly on the other side of the bed, but she reached out for my arm.

"She's going to be okay, mom," Leslie said as we both watched Gilly seizing. "She's going to be okay."

But Gilly wasn't coming out of her seizure as quickly as she had with previous seizures, a symptom of medicine withdrawal. Her breathing had become heavy and labored.

"Her color is changing," another nurse said with a sense of urgency.

Gilly's lips began to turn blue, her complexion turned paler.

"Please! Help her! Do something!" I screamed.

The doctors injected Ativan into her IV. Another asked for oxygen. Another checked to make sure her airway was cleared.

"Helpherhelpherhelpher," I wailed, begging, pleading.

"Clear her airway!" the doctor ordered the nurse who dove toward Gilly's clenched mouth.

It had happened so fast. Patrick was getting movies to watch. A friend texted me she had ordered chocolate chip cookies to be delivered for Gilly. Mike shared a joke that made Gilly squeal one of her trademark boisterous take-no-prisoners laugh as the EEG technologist wheeled in the monitor.

Now there were six people around my daughter furiously trying to keep her alive.

"Helpherhelpherhelpher" was all I could say as I cupped Gilly's cheek in my hand, praying for her to wake up. Please, Gilly, wake up. This was a seizure like no other, so violent in its consumption of the body it inhabited. Gilly's hospital bed shook in response to the epileptic earthquake. Leslie kept a firm grip on my arm as we both stood on opposite sides of Gilly's bed.

Gilly continued to contract, her chest raising in a marked rhythm. Up. Down. Up. Down.

"Gilly. Gilly," Mike cried from the foot of her bed. We had assumed our positions in battle, Mike at one end of the bed, me at the other, doctors and nurses in between. But I had nothing to fight with.

A hush covered the room for a second. Gilly's breathing slowly resumed a normal pattern. Soon the convulsions stopped.

"She's coming out," the doctor said, keeping his hand gently on Gilly's leg, not to restrain her, but as if to will her back into our world.

Gilly opened her eyes, blood dripping from her mouth onto the new two-piece pajamas I had bought for her the week before.

"Gilly? Do you know where you are?" the doctor asked gently.

Gilly nodded her head, staring and giving a sweet innocent smile.

"Hiiiiiii," Gilly said and smiled at the crowd around her bed.

"Hi," the doctor smiled as the other doctor and nurses quietly laughed at Gilly's tender response. "How are you? Do you know where you are?"

"Uh-huh," Gilly nodded, big-eyed, looking at everyone as if she had just landed on the planet earth for the first time. "I'm sorry. I don't know."

"Gilly, do you know who this is?" the doctor asked and pointed to me standing next to her.

Gilly nodded yes, but then said, "I don't know."

"How about him?" the doctor pointed toward Mike, standing at the end of the bed, tearfully smiling.

"Hi, Dada!" Gilly said to everyone's relief.

"So, who is this?" the doctor asked once again pointing to me. Gilly looked curiously at the crying woman in front of her.

"Is that the TV remote?" she asked wide-eyed and innocently.

"No, it's your mom," the doctor said as Leslie and I both rubbed Gilly's arms.

"Hiiii," Gilly said again, smiling looking around at her bedside crowd.

"Hi, Gilly," the lead doctor said with a big grin. Everyone chuckled.

"I think she is the sweetest post-ictal patient we've ever had," he added and patted Gilly's hand.

"She's the sweetest baby," Mike said quietly as his eyes welled with tears.

Within a few more minutes, Gilly realized who she was and that her mother was not actually a television remote. She began to cry.

"Did I have a seizure? Did they get it on video?" Gilly asked, intent to know if she had accomplished what we had come there for. She was determined to find an answer.

"It's okay, sweetie, it's over, it's over, it's over," I said rubbing her shoulder as the Ativan slowly dripped into her veins and gave her a much needed rest from her gallant fight.

I barely slept that night, sitting up on the couch while Mike slumped into the rocking chair as we took shifts staying awake. I only hoped the voice in the wall found the source of Gilly's seizures because I promised myself I would never put my daughter through this horrendous procedure again.

Leslie tiptoed into the room in the middle of the night and tapped me on the shoulder. As I stood, we embraced. I cried into her shoulder.

"I know," she whispered, "I know."

.   .   .   .   .   .

I thought the worse part of the EVU was behind us, but the doctors' rounds the next morning proved differently.

Gilly's neurologist wasn't there and he had become like family to us, like a kindred spirit to Gilly. From the moment they had met, four years earlier, their bond had been deep and true. Gilly's recent seizures had drawn them closer, forging a fearless team intent to get Gilly healthy. Anxious to see him and hear his interpretation of her seizure, Gilly knew she would have to wait until that evening when he would come by after his day of research and meeting with other patients.

Meanwhile, other white coats spilled into the room, offering their diagnosis from Gilly's seizure the night before. A nurse wheeled in a television screen on a rolling cart as one of the doctors spoke to the residents and explained his interpretation of the video recording. On the screen was a paused image of Gilly in her bed with the EEG technologist standing on one side and me on the other. My stomach tightened.

"I want to see it," Gilly said, sitting up in her bed. "I want to see the recording of my episode."

The lead doctor lowered his eyebrows, looking at Mike and then me.

"No, I don't think that's a good idea," I said to Gilly, angry the doctors would even bring the recording into the room.

"I want to see it," Gilly repeated firmly, her countenance serious and somber.

A nurse intervened.

"Honey, we watched it this morning before rounds. I don't think you want to see it," she said.

"I've never seen what I look like and I want to know," Gilly said, looking at Mike. He shook his head. I waited for the doctors to weigh in, but they just looked at Gilly and acknowledged she was, technically, an adult and had the right to see her own grand mal.

Was everyone here crazy? This was a very bad idea, I thought as my body started to shake.

"No, I can't," I said and my eyes stung from the gut-wrenching thought of re-watching a nightmare. "I can't watch it again." Trying not to cry, I rushed into the hallway and a nurse followed me.

"I understand," she said, tearing up. "Gilly's doctor and I watched it this morning so he could share his analysis this evening when he stops by. We both couldn't finish watching it. But we've seen this happen before with patients who want to better understand their condition."

As we stood in the hallway, I heard the television monitor turned on.

And Gilly's scream.

And my voice. The frantic plea of a mother begging someone to save her daughter. I started to cry again as the nurse held me in her arms, also crying. After a few minutes, another nurse came into the hallway and asked me to come back in the room. Gilly wanted to see me. When I opened the door, Gilly was red-faced, crying with Mike holding her hand. The doctors and nurses excused themselves.

"I'm so sorry, Mama," she said as tears rolled down her cheeks. "I didn't know. I didn't know what I looked like having a seizure. I'm so sorry. I made them stop. I didn't finish watching. I had no idea. I feel so badly for what I've put my family and friends through when I seize."

"Shhhhh. This isn't your fault," I said, rubbing her head. "You haven't done anything wrong."

"We're going to get you better," Mike said. His voice cracked.

Softly sobbing, Mike, Gilly and I embraced, releasing the beast from each of us.

·   ·   ·   ·   ·   ·

Returning home, we were armed with a new diagnosis—frontal partial epilepsy that turns into generalized epilepsy. Translated: Gilly's epilepsy had indeed evolved into two types, something that occurs in less than one percent of epileptics. Our family made an unspoken, but always present, pact to use this diagnosis for the good that could come from it by knowing the origin of Gilly's seizures. We could've dwelled on the rarity with which this condition happened, especially after being seizure-free for over two years. And, of all times, in the second month into her freshman year of college. But why go there?

Secretly, I did go there for about one minute. Then I reminded myself that Gilly could have been in Mexico when her condition changed. Could have been swimming in the Yucatan's deep, dark Cenotes. Could have been sleeping alone in her Mexican host mother's guest bedroom. All those "could-have's" erased my obsessing over what Gilly had actually been dealt with.

December was the month on seizure watch. Every day without a seizure was a victory. Gilly needed six weeks of distance between her last seizure. Then six more weeks. And so on. This was a marathon, not a sprint. We were informed better about her triggers, though sleep and hydration remained the top two along with avoiding excessive "screen time"—computers, phone, television. Her medicine regimen was intense, twelve pills daily, divided into three times a day.

"Calm and boring" was our theme for the month of holiday lights, sappy Christmas shows on television, and hot chocolate. Her new medicine, the powerhouse Carbatrol, had some nasty side effects we were also advised to watch for, namely a dangerous drop in sodium. But this was also the new drug that worked effectively against frontal seizures. And so we watched.

We ate well, too. My friends set up nightly dinners brought to our house with love and disposable dishes so all we had to do was feed our hunger and care for Gilly. Her trundle bed's extra mattress was next to us in our master bedroom, which had become our hangout, watching Hallmark Christmas romance movies (spoiler: the guy always gets the girl), playing card games, reading and listening to music. Gilly also worked to complete her college classes, determined to finish the semester as she had begun it back in August, enthusiastically. Yet the strong cocktail of medicine was doing a number on her brain and body, effecting her cognitive abilities and her energy. But she would not give up.

"Honey, I'm sure we can get either medical withdrawal or incompletes so you can finish your classes for winter semester," I said one morning in our bedroom as Gilly was sitting on her mattress, typing on her computer in between taking frequent medicine-induced naps.

"I can do this," Gilly said with laser focus on her keyboard. "I don't want to quit. I just have to write a few more papers and take a final exam in my biology class."

I have no idea how we're going to get you to a final exam in Gainesville when you can barely stay awake longer than two hours at a time, I thought, but did not say. Instead I refilled her tumbler of ice water, readjusted her pillow and found a comfy spot to sit on the carpet next to Gilly's make-shift bed, my shoulder lightly touching hers, rising and lifting in unison to the steady, peaceful rhythm of her breathing.

Chapter 19

Her Room: A Universe in Blue

As Gilly slept beside me on her mattress by our bed, I wrote the following letter, one I never sent, but kept just in case.

December 2015

Professors of Gillian Rae Mangan
University of Florida
Gainesville, Florida

Dear Professors,

I'm in my daughter's bedroom, sitting on a white slip-covered chair next to her desk that has more books, pens, framed pictures, saffron scented candles and stationery than clear space. I'd sit on her daybed, but it's full, too, with pillows of all shapes and sizes, soft blankets and stuffed animals. She painted this room a light, dusty baby blue, saying this was her favorite color of all the bedrooms she's lived in, which is quite something considering she's lived in seven homes. But I must tell you she said the same thing about her lime green wall in the apartment and the bold navy and lavender stripes in the gray rental house and the hot pink walls in another. We couldn't afford paint for the tri-level rental, but Gilly said she would have picked her bedroom's pale beige walls that had been painted by the previous renters, if she could have.

So this is Gilly, making the best out of any situation she's in.

Her given name is Gillian Rae Mangan, my only daughter, born into our family with a brother two years older and an instantly smitten father who, seeing her for the first time in the hospital, tearfully said she would forever be his sweet baby doll. My obstetrician added by declaring we were now "an All American family," proud parents of a handsome son and a beautiful girl. I turned to my husband and smiled, recognizing our good fortune by saying, "Aren't we lucky?"

But, luck is a word I've come to use sparingly in the years that followed. Don't get me wrong—every single hour of every single day, I inhale a prayer of gratitude that Gillian Rae Mangan graces my world. She's extraordinary, another word I don't use often, but she truly is, possessing more resilience, determination and heart than I could have possibly imagined. And, well, that's just it, because these things that define my incredibly resilient, determined and big-hearted daughter have been tested again and again. She hasn't been as lucky as I would have hoped. As any mother wishes for her children.

You've noticed this already, right? She's in your class, the eager blue-eyed, blonde freshman sitting in the front row who introduced herself to you on the first day. Who wore Chaco sandals to class with a sixteen-ounce tumbler of water practically attached to her. Who asked follow-up questions and showed you her homework before she turned it in. Who called me exclaiming, "I love my classes! It's amazing what I'm learning!"

Who has come to be known as Gilly, which I bet is what she asked you to call her, a nickname lovingly given to her many years ago when she was a toddler— maybe by me or her brother or maybe it was her Pre-K teacher who said she had to stay on her toes to keep up with Gilly Girl.

Who laughs the loudest, smiles the biggest and hugs the longest, not letting go of her embrace until it's absolutely necessary.

Who has notified you more than once by email at three a.m. of her impending absence as an intravenous pic line ran anti-seizure medicine through her vein in the emergency room. Who followed up to make sure you received her homework that she turned in on time even though you graciously gave her a few more days. Who refused to ask for extra time to take her mid-term exams as she was fighting uncontrollable seizures that rendered her a "wet noodle" as she recovered from grand mals that doctors equated to running a twenty-six mile marathon. Every. Single. Seizure.

Which brings me to why I'm writing to you. Final exam week is approaching. Even though Gilly is registered with the Student Disability Office granting her an extension for completing her fall semester of classes, she wants to finish her classes on time like your other students. Yet certainly you know by now, she isn't like your other students. But heavens be damned if Gilly will let this stop her! So, I'm going along with my daughter's self-imposed mission to ask you for consideration to grant Gilly her wish to let her submit any unfinished work that she missed when she was hospitalized. She'd also like to take your final exams on a day during exam week when I can drive her to campus.

I understand why this is important to her. No offense, but it's really not about the significance of your class or the subject matter at hand. Rather, it's about Gilly finding some small sliver of normalcy in the crappy deck of cards she's been dealt. I mean, really, can you think of anything more horrifying as a nineteen-year-old going off to college than convulsing unconsciously on the floor in front of your peers? Requiring someone to be with you at all times including when you take a shower? Having to ask someone to drive you because you lost that privilege the first time pools of drool and blood formed around your mouth and indicated the dreaded monster of epilepsy had returned? Religiously taking your twelve pills every twelve hours no matter what?

I'm sure you get the picture. And if you don't, I just wish you were sitting here with me because a picture is worth a thousand words, but in Gilly's room, a thousand words paint the picture. Gilly must have over one hundred thousand words spilling out of every corner of the room which is just how she likes it. Authors like F. Scott Fitzgerald, Ian McEwan, Stephen King, John Green, Harper Lee line her bookshelves, fill her baskets beneath her desk and lie open-faced on her bed. And the literary goddess of them all, Jane Austen, is everywhere. On Gilly's totes, wall plaques, notecards and bound in the books of her favorites— Pride and Prejudice, Sense and Sensibility and Persuasion. A framed poem of Ted Kooser hangs just outside her bedroom door. She made an interpretative collage of the Nebraskan poet's "After Years" for an eighth-grade class assignment and captured Kooser's lament of watching his universe unfold without having anyone to share it with.

Her rainbow-colored woven hammock from her Mexico study abroad trip is on the floor, waiting to be hung, which we will do soon. Gilly said she wants to nap in it once she can sleep alone. But for now she sleeps in our room on a mattress next to our bed until the seizure coast is clear and who knows when that will be? No one. Not me. Not Gilly. Not you. And yet, Gilly tells me she is happy with who she is, not giving into her condition, instead living her life, loving her friends and family and writing in her blog, Finding Faces, chronicling her condition and giving hope to those who read it.

. *A black-fabric journal sits on Gilly's desk with the quote, "With freedom, books, flowers and the moon, who could not be happy?"*

If fighting through adversity and loving through the pain is what it means to be an All-American family, maybe we fall into this innocuous description. Who the hell knows? More importantly, I hope you have come to realize what I already know: we are all so very lucky to know and love Gilly. To watch the universe through her eyes and her wide-open heart is a gift.

Thank you for your consideration to offer Gilly a kindness I know, without a doubt, she would give to you.

Most sincerely,
Gilly's Mom

Chapter 20

The Master Bedroom: This Side Up

A refined master bedroom is complete when it includes what matters most, a family. So wrote a woman I once knew, the woman I once was, sitting in my fancy chair for the editor's page in *The Style Book*. I found the seven-year-old book hidden behind paperbacks and hardbacks on my shelf while searching for a novel that Gilly and I could read aloud together so we could honor her neurologist's admonition to have a "calm and boring" December after leaving the hospital. Time could be our friend for each day that rest and a potent mix of medicine prevented a seizure for Gilly. My company—now Mike's company, too—was steadfastly supportive, covering work obligations when needed, networking for the best medical opinions in the country, and sending us a very large basket of blankets, puzzles, books and board games with a note reminding us this should be a season of caring for our family. I took much of the month off from work. Mike took vacation time, too. Time for Gilly to, hopefully, heal. Time for us to just be.

And time for Gilly and me to find a good book to get lost in for a little while. But I was transfixed at the moment on the book in front of me. Thumbing through the pages of my published homage to domesticity, I thought about how much I'd changed since fretting over chapters about bathroom fixtures and bedroom furniture and ambient light in a hallway. How home had come to mean so much more to me than an optimal paint color. Actually, home had come to mean more about less than about more. Less stuff. Less aesthetic emphasis on décor and table settings and floral arrangements. Yet reading that voice on the page—*my* voice from what seemed a lifetime ago—elicited an unexpected response, one that wrapped me in warmth the same way I felt when I drank a steaming cup of milky hot chocolate on a cold night. I no longer felt remorse for what I had lost, or pity for my naïve observations about whatever I thought was important at that time. Rather I felt compassion for the forty-two-year-old woman writing about the celebration of what it had meant to be home. I didn't get it all right back then. Massive Victorian headboards did not make a style comeback. And fresco-styled painting of cherub angels on a ceiling over a tub was simply *de mauvais gout*. But I empathized with what a younger me was shooting for, contentment. Exactly what many American families had hoped and dreamed and worked their asses for back then and still desired, even if they were broken and weary from the financial unrest of the past turbulent years. Peace. Home. Security. Love washed over me for *The Style Book* editor staring at me with a face absent of crow's feet holding onto her piece of history a la Will Durant. Oh, honey, if you only knew what the next seven years would bring you.

But I didn't know. And I remained uncertain about what the next seven years would bring—hell, the next seven days, seven minutes. All I knew was what was right in front of me, my husband, my daughter and my son, home from college. And my bedroom that had become my haven of comfort, my refuge from the unknown. It was an addition the homeowners had built connecting the original structure to a solarium, game room, walk-in storage unit and a master bedroom with his-and-her bathrooms. Nylon cream-colored pile wall-to-wall carpet covered the floor with dark stained beams hugging the ceiling. Our queen-sized bed buffeted the wall with Gilly's spare mattress beside it. Those first few weeks I ended up sleeping on the floor next to Gilly as if I could better respond if a seizure should occur.

Christmas was a week away, yet I couldn't resist giving Griffin and Gilly one present early, matching "dancing water speakers" with bright-colored LED light-infused water that bounced up and down to the beat of the music, kind of like the water fountain at The Bellagio in Vegas.

"Let's connect them to my phone," Gilly said as she pulled the plastic speakers out of the box and plugged them into her cell phone app of music. Bursts of bright blue, green, red and pink water shot up like a mini geyser to the pulsing bass of a Justin Timberlake song.

Since our bedroom was Hibernation Central, Gilly and I added some holiday festivity to it. We hung tiny, white, star-shaped Christmas tree lights on the wall above her floor mattress, making an illuminated smile over her head. Then we draped an extra set of the lights on my bed's headboard, secured by good old fashioned duct tape, a design element that definitely wouldn't have made the cut for *The Style Book*.

One night we turned off the overhead light, leaving on the starburst necklaces of light above our beds. Gilly turned on her water speakers and picked some classic favorites for Mike and Griffin, who had joined us on the floor by Gilly's mattress to play a card game.

"Welcome to Club Mangan," I laughed while shuffling and dealing cards to each player in the dimly lit room. We played "just one more round" of games that turned into many more rounds, got tickled at silly jokes and our favorite movie lines from *Oh Brother, Where Art Thou?*

"Hey, you won!" Gilly said, giggling. "You're bona fide!"

"You've got prospects!" Mike echoed.

"She's a suitor!" Griffin added.

And we offered our opinions about what was the best Beatles song ever as the water speaker flickered colorful boom-boom-boom drops to Paul, Ringo and John's electric guitar riff in "Revolution." For a few hours we shut out the world looming behind our closed door, a world of grand mals, insulin injections, one-year home leases, and medical bills. I do not remember ever feeling as whole as I did that night at Club Mangan, sitting on the carpeted floor with who mattered most to me, my family.

· · · · · ·

I got married the following weekend. It was a last-minute decision after driving home from dinner downtown. The only guests were Griffin and Gilly, who were in the car with Mike and me. We pulled over to a vacant lot for our ad hoc ceremony. Mike didn't turn off the car. Instead, he switched on his hazard lights and left the driver's door open (maybe a for a quick pre-wedding jitters escape?) It may have been the shortest wedding ever, except for one technicality. We were already married.

Which is why we decided to do it all over again.

December marked our twenty-fifth year of marriage, a milestone that reassured and confounded me. There is beauty in longevity and shared history and I had always been a big fan of both. But, man oh man, there's that unknowing part of a relationship. If, many years ago, I'd have seen the Mangan Marriage Spoiler Trailer of challenges Mike and I would face, I would have put down my large bag of buttered popcorn, sprinted back to the ticket booth and demanded a showing of the Nora Ephron version of us. Not the one Francis Ford

Coppola would have directed, all dark and ominous with sad violin music playing in the background. Give me light and happy, I would demand! With an upbeat soundtrack. And Tom Hanks and Meg Ryan.

Yet, that's not the real world or a real marriage. Here was the part that confounded me after twenty-five years—the real parts of being together had become the very heart of what made us, well, us. When we were scared and worried and stressed. When reality hit us square in the eyes. When we retreated to our respective corners in muted resignation that today would not be a good day to figure out the questions of life. And when we would meet in the middle to acknowledge nobody else was going to save us better than ourselves. We found a way. Sometimes not always the best way. Sometimes not harmoniously. God knows, I was thankful for the happy times. Yet when the weight of the world was sitting on top of my chest, I found comfort in knowing that Mike was beside me to hold the anvil of anxiety for a while.

We had continued to have our share of hard. But we woke up every day, finding a way to get through the difficult and inhaling deep, long breaths of the easy when it came along. And the easy part was Griffin and Gillian. Always. We were mindful of the gifts of our children along with a network of family and friends in a community of love like nothing I'd experienced anywhere else.

And we had each other.

Dinner downtown had been a rare treat, a perfect time for an anniversary celebration, Mike said. I wore a new black tee-shirt dress a friend had brought to my home from a store where she worked along with a few other outfits for my slimmed down figure. I'd lost twenty pounds since September, an effect of the unsolicited stress diet I was on while caring for Gilly. Not the way I would recommend losing weight, but my post-menopausal body welcomed the absence of my usual belly fat. Now that my face wasn't round and puffy, I cut my hair short in a pixie-style, joking it was my Justin Bieber look. Mike loved it. I liked it too. I felt stronger with my short hair, free, liberated.

On the drive home, Mike turned down a street to show the children the church where we were married. A fire had claimed First Baptist Church decades ago. All that was left was the vacant property. It took about a second for us to decide a wedding was in order. We hopped out of the car, laughing like school kids. Griffin walked me down the grassy aisle as Gilly and Mike waited in the middle of the lot. Holding hands, Mike and I shared what it meant to be married to each other.

"I, Mike Mangan, take thee, Amy Mangan..."

"...with the Justin Bieber haircut," I interrupted.

"With the Justin Bieber haircut," Mike added with a big grin.

"To keep being my lawfully-wedded wife in sickness or in health, for richer or poorer, but we're totally cool if we have a little more rich in our lives," Mike said chuckling as he squeezed my hand. "But, all joking aside, it doesn't matter what we have as long as we have each other."

Mike's eyes welled with tears while Griffin and Gilly stood close by. Cars slowly drove past us to stare briefly at the family in the field.

"And, I, Amy Mangan, take thee, Mike Mangan..."

"With the George Clooney haircut," Mike added.

"With the George Clooney haircut that I still think is too short," I said.

"Be nice," Mike mockingly joked. "It's our wedding."

"To keep being my lawfully-wedded husband in sickness or health, for richer or poorer, for more foot massages and viewing rights to the TV..."

"Hey, I didn't ask for that," Mike quipped.

"You had your chance, mister."

"'Till death do us part—which I hope is a very long time from now because I have so much more I want to share with you," I said suddenly overcome with emotion. "So much we need to make up for. I do love you, Mike Mangan, for as long as we both shall live and then some."

"I love you, too, sweetheart," Mike said and we both cried, shedding tears for the recognition of what we'd been through since we'd last stood at that very spot a quarter of a lifetime earlier.

"We now pronounce you husband and wife!" Griffin and Gilly said in unison.

As Mike and I kissed, I looked up and saw a shooting star in the chilly, star-lit sky. But it was actually an airplane.

Just like a Nora Ephron movie. Almost.

•   •   •   •   •   •

The new year brought a new normal for the Mangan household. Griffin returned to Tallahassee with a CGM, a continuous glucose monitor, to better control his diabetes through a tiny sensor inserted under his skin that continuously checked glucose levels in the tissue. A transmitter sent info from the sensor to a pager-like wireless monitor that was shared on a cell phone app, meaning Mike and I would be alerted along with Griffin if he had a sugar low or high. This, in combination with Gilly's diligent text updates from Gainesville when she took her meds, when she took a shower, when she went to bed, allowed me to rest easier, as contradictory as that might have seemed.

Gilly returned home for long weekends of rest and quiet. A low sodium level was caught from routine blood work while Gilly was with us one Saturday morning in January, leading us to rush to the hospital to confirm what we had begun to fear. Carbatrol, the medicine that had been the only drug effective in preventing her seizures, was dangerously lowering her sodium. Her doctor immediately switched her to a "newer family member" of the medicine called Tegratol that, after a few weeks, revealed to be equally powerful in keeping the beast away. Crisis averted for the time being, I thought, wondering how many more of these we could handle, that *she* could handle.

By April, it was evident Gilly could handle more than humanly possible. Pushing herself through her daily routine of medicine to maintain a full load of classes at the university, Gilly continued her life of fierce determination, which I believed to be her Herculean secret weapon that had kept her emotionally sane for the previous seven months. But I was reminded that Gilly still harbored the desires of a nineteen-year-old college girl. Like wanting go on her sorority's big out-of-town dance to celebrate the end of the school year. And climb the Sierra Madrid mountains with her fellow Lombardi Scholars for their overseas summer trip. Mike, her doctor and I all assured her she would be able to do these things one day, but not yet. Most of the time, she accepted our response. When she didn't, I reminded myself how grateful I was we had this kind of argument. I thought of the children whom we had met in the Epilepsy Video Unit floor who would give anything to argue with their parents about such things. Children whose epilepsy could not be controlled with medicine.

What I wasn't grateful for was that we had to find a new rental on top of establishing a payment plan for the myriad of medical bills that began to arrive in our mailbox each day. Another move meant more money down the drain for first and last month security deposits, but I kept the worry demon at bay, better than I had before. All I had to do was look at Griffin's glucose number on my cell phone or read Gilly's medicine update text to set me straight that what I was facing was manageable. That much I had learned.

"Let's see if we can stay here one more year," Mike said one night after dinner as we sat in the living room facing the park. Hard to believe we had lived there for over two years. "I know it's not ideal, but it would make sense if we could."

Even though I craved finding a home of my own—a dream I couldn't shake—I knew Mike's suggestion was the best option.

"I agree. Why don't you make that call?" I said cleaning the dishes. "I have to re-order Griffin's CGM sensors before he runs out."

I should have taken the rent extension assignment. My call to the CGM vendor lasted a frustrating two hours without any resolution. First, I was put on hold so I could be transferred to refill orders and I listened to elevator-type music for thirty-five minutes. When I was able to speak to a human, I was informed that Griffin's order actually belonged in a different department and I was transferred, and then put on hold again. By the time I spoke to the young man who informed me this was his first month on the job, it was nearing eight o'clock at night, five p.m. mountain time, where the new-man-on-the-job said he wouldn't be able to process the order now that it was quitting time.

"Are you kidding me?" I asked. "I've been talking to your company for the past two hours."

"I'm sorry, ma'am. I understand your frustration, but the person I need to talk to in order to confirm this order has already left for the day," he said in monotone voice.

Hanging up, I texted Griffin to see how many sensors he had left.

None, he replied. The last one just died.

Griffin would not go to sleep with the CGM backup that night. Which meant I would not go to sleep. We made a mother-son pact Griffin would text me throughout the night to share his finger-pricked glucose number. A diabetic's worst fear is falling into a sugar low or high coma, many of which commonly occur at night. A diabetic mother's worst fear is her out-of-town son falling so low or rising so high that her only response is calling emergency dispatch three hours away while also hoping one of his roommates is close by to give him a juice box or glucose tabs or, worse, a Glucagon injection. And Griffin's randomly assigned roommate in his apartment was less than responsive, usually gone most nights partying.

Griffin kept his end of the deal, texting me his BG—blood glucose—numbers throughout the night.

Day Two. I called the vendor again first thing in the morning before I headed to work. I had to wait, however, for their offices to open, Utah-time. Once again I held for over half an hour and once again, I was given another reason Griffin's order could not be processed. Didn't have the doctor's ninety-day refill order. Wish I would have known this piece of information the night before. Hanging up with the vendor, I then called the doctor who immediately sent the order.

Night Two. Griffin texted me his BG a few times throughout the night. I hoped he'd fall back asleep, even though I could not in the hours in between his texts, no matter how many real estate listings I scanned online to try to dull my brain from a mother's worry.

Day Three. I took a half day off from work, anticipating another long round of calls to the vendor, the only approved provider my health insurance would pay for. This time the new guy reluctantly took my call and told me he would place the order, but it would be approximately three to four days until Griffin would receive his sensors. When I pushed to have them over-nighted, he succumbed. Victory.

Night Three. Griffin and I texted each other and Mike served as back up, increasingly concerned about his wife's unsolicited participation in what appeared to be a macabre sleep deprivation study. So, I fell asleep eating dinner...no big deal. But every time Mike's phone buzzed a text message from Griffin, I woke up.

Day Four. No package yet, Griffin texted.

Night Four. Mike and I took turns checking on Griffin, who reminded me there were diabetics in the world who didn't have CGMs. Yes, I know, I said, and I wish they could have them. I refrained from reminding Griffin how several times Mike and I had to wake him up by phone, alerting him to a dangerous BG number so low—lower than fifty-five (a normal BG is one hundred and twenty)—that the CGM app on my phone simply alerted as "LOW."

Day Five, Six, Seven, and Eight. Repeated calls to the vendor can't explain why Griffin's sensors had yet to arrive. A week and a half after my initial call, I insisted to speak to the management. New guy wasn't too keen on this request.

"Look, ma'am, I'm sorry this has happened, but you know your son does have options," he said smugly.

"Oh, really? Can you please tell me what they are?" I asked, biting my upper lip in anger.

"Well, he can always prick his finger to check his blood glucose."

"Yes, I'm aware of that procedure, which generally works best when a diabetic isn't sleeping, as his sugar drops so low that he doesn't wake up. And if he doesn't wake up, he can't prick his finger," I said firmly, feeling my whole body shake.

"I understand. But you have to understand we will need to do a new order for Griffin's sensors and I'm not sure I can overnight them the second time because our system doesn't let us," he said.

By now, I was seething, ready to pull the new guy through the phone and slap his smug little new employee face.

"Sir, are you a diabetic?" I asked after taking a long, deep breath.

"No, I am not," he said.

"Do you have children who are diabetics or anyone you love who is a diabetic?"

"No, I do not."

"Then I'd like to offer you a constructive suggestion as you begin your career in this field," I said as tears rolled down my cheeks. "Act like you are a diabetic. Act like someone you love is a diabetic. Walk in our shoes. Really, go there. A little empathy would go a long way because neither my son nor I have gotten a full night's sleep in the past week and even when he gets his sensors, he will never get a full night's sleep again, but the rest he can get will be better because he has the CGM as a back-up. Do you understand now?"

"I do," he said quietly as I heard his fingers tapping on his keyboard to request an overnight shipment of sensors for Griffin. Hanging up the phone, I sat on the couch in my home office and stared out the sliding glass window and watched a woodpecker bash his bill against a pine tree.

My phone pinged. Gilly sent me a text.

I'D LIKE YOU TO READ A PAPER I WROTE FOR ONE OF MY CLASSES. JUST EMAILED IT TO YOU. LOVE YOU.

For a minute, I contemplated laying my head on the couch's armrest. A quick nap was just within my reach. Instead, I grabbed my laptop and clicked onto the email from Gilly.

It was her eulogy.

Swallowing hard, I began to read my daughter's somber tribute to herself, assigned by her human spirituality and health professor, a teacher who had shown great empathy for Gilly's condition, checking on her by email and always making sure she had a ride back to her dorm. In class he pushed her to expand her impressions of self, to ask honest and open questions about her health, both physical and spiritual. Through the semester, when Gilly had shared her papers with me, I could see a marked development in her writing and comprehension. She was blooming into a mature and inquisitive young writer and woman. I hit print on the keyboard, thinking I should save a copy.

This poignantly written paper, with metaphors befitting a young poet, hit me hard as I read each paragraph memorializing her life and acknowledging those who had been important to her. That's so like her, I thought, spotlighting the goodness of others when the assignment's intent was really about her. She thanked her friends for getting her through the rough patches. She wrote of her dad's gentleness and constant love and support that had sustained her throughout her life.

Then she wrote about me.

Twice I re-read her sentences, processing the sentiment in front of me on my computer screen as my eyes began to sting.

Whatever generosity in spirit she had shown for others in her eulogy, Gilly turned off the love spigot when she got to her mother. She wrote how she hoped I would accept the choices she had made. That I would not judge her. That I would see her as she really was. I'm paraphrasing here. I didn't give myself enough time to memorize Gilly's Notes on a Shrill Mother because I slammed the laptop shut and threw it on the couch so hard I startled Honey, sleeping next to me.

This is what she thinks of me?

Some judgmental mother harshly critical of her daughter's choices? When did I become *that*? Was it before or after the encouragement I'd text her each morning to tell her how proud I was of her as she woke up to face each day with courage and kindness? Or after the six weeks in the fall that I had spent working out of a Gainesville hotel room, fielding projects and meetings for work while remaining on call to help Gilly when she needed me? Maybe it was when I was managing her medical care with mind-numbing conversations with her doctors and nurses about the next complicated step in the plan to heal Gilly? Yes, I had told her I was the charter member of Team Gilly and had enlisted her friends to give me their cell phones and to take my cell phone number and to keep a copy of the medical emergency procedure I had typed out for them.

Honest to God, I don't know when I would have had time to judge her. I was too busy trying to keep her alive. If I thought back, I remembered she wasn't happy with something I'd said the week before, when Gilly had been home for the weekend. Although is was innocuous and the argument would pass, I recalled her stony look of contempt and the way it froze us from talking after I told her what I thought. Even my optimistic daughter struggled with the limitations of living with a life-threatening condition and it was wearing on the both of us.

"Life right now seems like a constant stream of 'No's," Gilly said to me after I had put the kibosh on something she wanted to do like mountain climbing in June.

Yet did that one incident mean that I should be punished while Mike got an Academy Award–type shout-out for his constant support? Of course he loved his daughter. I would never question that. But I also never saw him calling the hospital to ask for copies of Gilly's EEG and MRI and blood work. Not once did he share her records with other neurologists that I had networked to find for a second and third opinion. Nor did he make a binder four inches thick tracking every conversation about, appointment, medical note, and prescription for Gilly. And I'm pretty sure I was the one who spent every week in the hotel save for two days which Mike took and even then I had to call the front desk for them to send someone to his room, knocking loudly on the door to tell him that Gilly had suffered another seizure and that I was already half way between home and the emergency room. When he got to the ER, Mike said he hadn't had the volume turned up on his cell phone when he took a shower. Shocker. Of course he didn't. Every night, I slept next to my bedside table with the phone on. *Always.*

I returned to my laptop and Gilly's eulogy.

"As part of my last days, I would tell my mom how I have appreciated her advice over the past years yet do not want to falter in her shadow," Gilly wrote. "I would ask mom why she criticized me so frequently and if she would remember me brightly."

Resentment spread into my chest, filling up a hollow cavity with despair and spite. How ugly, I thought, as I fought to attack the toxic malice enveloping my being. There was more, something about us both being bright and how she loved me though she needed to place her happiness first. All this because I told her she couldn't go to a dance or climb a mountain after being hospitalized? Such is the push-pull of a mother-daughter relationship, let alone a mother-daughter relationship fueled by a health crisis. I chose to ignore the other parts of the eulogy where she was kind about our relationship.

I had to get out of the house. I ended up driving on the highway, reprimanding the universe with each mile that distanced me from home to a mucky lake a county away, drawing me closer, though I didn't originally know where I was going. I only knew where I had been. Several times I howled in the car, crying to no one but myself. My head throbbed as I reached the conclusion I had done everything wrong. All those years I had convinced myself that my family and I were fighters who could get through anything because we were the Mangans. We weren't quitters. We were loved and we gave love. And I was an imperfect, but decent mother, wife and daughter.

"Who am I kidding?" I screamed into the steering wheel as I pulled into a remote gas station on the edge of the lake to use the bathroom. I had no plan for what I would do next, but I had to pee. Even my dramatic exit was flawed. I paid a dollar and sixty-nine cents for a diet soda, my penance for using the facilities. When I got back in the car, I looked at my watch. It was seven o'clock. I had been gone for two hours. I looked at my phone. Two text messages from Gilly, both asking if I was okay. As if she knew. How the hell could she not know after sharing her paper? And three text messages from Mike.

ARE YOU COMING HOME SOON?

EVERYTHING OK?

HONEY?

Staring at the screen, I had to buy a little more time.

I'M NOT SURE I'M COMING BACK. I'M TIRED.

Then I disconnected the Life 360 phone app that tracked where I was. Who cared where I was? I pulled out of the parking lot of the gas station and turned north. Toward Orange Lake.

Until this point I'd driven in silence, but I longed to hear something else beside the bitterness and regret that consumed my car. I turned on the radio and the Sirius Broadway channel lit up in neon green letters "SECRET GARDEN: HOW COULD I EVER KNOW." Resisting the urge to change the channel, I kept my eye on the road in front of me as a soprano voice sang in desperate remorse after realizing she had to leave, she had to go, even though someone still needed her so.

Clear eyed, I drove down the empty road devoid of any sign of life. No more tears. I was all dried up. Kind of like Orange Lake, which was lower than I'd remembered. I kept driving. All the while thinking how very tired I was. And surprised.

I was shocked by my actions. I thought I'd gotten through the worse part.

Comparatively speaking, everyone was healthy, well, by Mangan terms, of course. Mike and I both had jobs. A roof over our heads. A marriage finally back on track. So, why now? Why this?

My cell phone rang. It was Mike. I let it go to voice mail. Mike sent a text.

PLEASE COME HOME. GRIFFIN, GILLY AND I LOVE YOU.

When I was little, Dad and I would drive to the lake, usually on the way to Gainesville before a Gator football game. His excuse for the detour was to "hear the pre-game radio show," but it didn't air outside of the car after we had stepped out onto the soft grassy lip of the lake to stand, his waist to my shoulder, in silent reverie and in awe of the scene in front of us. The blue sky blended into the lake's mirrored top, still, silent, quiet. Dad shared the last of the boiled peanuts we had bought on the road thirty miles earlier.

"It doesn't get much prettier than this," Dad said, squeezing me into the crook of his hip.

What would Dad think of me right now, I wondered, as I turned off the highway and found the two-lane road that would take me parallel to the lake. What would he think of his daughter running away from home?

"I'm sorry, Dad," I cried as the lake came into view.

I parked on someone's private property, trespassing with my car of remorse. The lights were off in the cement block house that was next to the lake. All I needed to do was drive.

My phone rang again. I turned it off and hit the accelerator straight for the lake, the most impetuous decision I could ever remember making in my life. So unlike me, Amy Yeary Mangan, the responsible one, who when friends would shake their head telling me how strong I was through everything I'd been through, I'd toss my head back and say, "I'm just doing what anyone would do in a situation like this."

In a situation where my family lived a two-alarm life, our young adult children still tethered to their parents for safekeeping. Where we bought medical identification bracelets in bulk. Buy one, get one free, right, I'd joke, laughing off the pain that retreated for a little while. Where our paychecks never seemed to be enough. Where our savings remained deficient from breaking the perpetual and costly rental cycle.

Where, lately, I had kept running into glass doors in my house, rushing to get to the next place, winding up with a blue-black bruised forehead on more than one occasion. I was equally as skittish as I was frenetic, jumping at the sound of the refrigerator's ice maker dumping ice into its bin and making a crushing thud like Gilly's fall on her bathroom floor. Clutching my chest to compress the thump-thump of my tachycardia heart when the radio newscaster announced Wall Street had a lackluster week with declining stocks. Leaping from my bed when the CGM alarm announced in a doorbell chime Griffin's low blood sugar alert. Holding my breath when Mike would call to say he had a bad day. Bad as in lost your job or you have too many emails?

Enough.

As I pressed my foot down on the accelerator, my tires began to spin, throwing mud like a kitchen beater out of control. I put the car in park. When I changed gears back to drive, the car wouldn't move. I was stuck. The more I hit the gas, the more bogged down I became.

"Really?" I yelled. "This is the best I can do?"

The sun set, dimming the sky's lights, as the water blurred into the air above it and I sat in my car, stuck by the lake, captive by show tunes. Even Shakespeare wouldn't have known what to do with this scenario. My head was pulsing to the beat of the music on the radio as I opened my purse to find a migraine pill that I washed down with the last of my diet soda. Taking a deep breath, I turned on the inside light of my car to find my cell phone, which had fallen beneath my feet. Turning the phone back on, I played Mike's messages.

"Honey, I know it is hard. I'll do whatever I can to make it easier. Please call me. I love you."

"I'm just checking on you. I saw Gilly's paper on your printer. She didn't mean it. You've got to know that. Griffin, Gillian love their mama and I love you."

"Little Shop of Horrors" musical started to play from the car speakers. Crying as I turned off the radio, I thought how funny Mike and Griffin and Gillian would find this predicament that their mother had gotten herself into if it weren't so damn serious. How we would laugh about it for months to come because, honestly, life really can be stranger than stand-up comedy. Laughter had so often insulated us from the elements of reality. The hard gentle of a well-worn family.

"Please come home," Mike quietly pleaded in his last message.

I leaned my head back on the headrest as tears rolled down my cheeks and poured out of my eyes, my whole body, it seemed, enough to fill up the lake basin in front of me. Maybe it had a hole inside of it that kept it from staying full. I wept in the blackness that surrounded me.

All along I thought I had handled my struggles like I was supposed to, possessed to stay wired for survival. To keep moving amidst the unsettled debris of my life. To push forward without stopping. Without pausing to check and make sure I had enough fuel inside of me for the long drive. Helpless wasn't in my vocabulary. Sometimes I had accepted fear for more than it needed to be. It had dictated my instinctive reaction to draw everything and everyone closer. But in doing so, I closed off a part of me. The part that still yearned to be in the mystery of my future instead of trapped in the constant present battle of crisis. Oh, how I wanted to explore who I could still be. Yet, the fatigue of always fighting overcame me. I closed my eyes.

My body washed warm as I drifted into silence. Images floated by. Mike wrapping his arm around my waist when we danced after dinner in the foyer of the last home we owned. Griffin holding my hand as the opening credits rolled to "The West Wing." Gillian pouring batter into the mixing bowl to make our annual Fourth of July cake, holding the spatula up and asking, in a lilting Ina Garten voice, "How easy was that?" My sisters packing garbage bags of my earthly possessions like a well-run manufacturing line. Mama decorating her home with her Christmas bunny for Valentine's Day. Daddy grabbing my red tool box from the back of his pick-up at a construction site. Friends bringing sustenance in food, comfort, packing tape and prayers.

And a photo from a soft-bound publication with limited distribution of a middle-aged woman holding on tight to her history so as not to lose it.

I cried for the love that had always been around me. I cried for the love I tried to give back in some small way of showing gratitude for the people whose love I had never lost. And I let go of no longer giving myself permission to stop. And pause. And rest. I didn't have to fix all that was broken. I only needed to repair the fragile parts of me that had earned a well-deserved rest.

Taking a deep breath, I put the car in reverse and slowly and gently pressed on the accelerator. The car jerked back, then forth, then back, gaining traction to pull out of the hole I was in. Staring into the darkness in front of me, I put the car in drive and turned away from the lake.

An hour later I was home. Mike opened the back door before my car was completely pulled in. As I got out of the car, he hugged me, crying in my ear as I quietly sobbed into his chest.

"I love you," Mike said softly. "I'm so glad you're home."

Later Mike would take the night shift to check on Griffin. I would sleep an entire eight hours. The next morning, Mike greeted me with a hot cup of coffee before he folded the laundry. He always did the laundry. And the dishes. And made the children's lunches when they were in middle and high school when he was working from home, and after, when he wasn't. PB&J sandwiches on whole wheat with fruit and a three-by-five sized note to wish Griffin and Gilly a good day. He carried us even when I was too busy fighting on the hill of survival to notice. I wasn't the only soldier.

For the next few weeks, I continued to sleep well, restoring the crumbled parts inside me. No longer did I fall asleep in constant worry if my son or my daughter was okay. There were still moments of fear, there always would be, but I learned the importance of balancing my vulnerabilities with my victories. And I had plenty.

And I had Mike. He'd been there all along. But our bedroom, from the last dark days in Oak Lane to the Park View cave of safety, always had someone else present.

The ghost of John Thain.

I'd stayed in touch with the object of my disgust. He'd done well after his brief stint at Merrill Lynch before it shattered the lives of its non-executive employees, trusting investors and optimistic citizens, the latter who worked hard and cared for their families with the hope of fulfilling the American Dream, of having the opportunity to succeed regardless of class or circumstances. Thain took his million dollar severance package and found a new executive position as CEO of CIT Group. In a 2015 interview with a banking magazine, Thain defended his role at Merrill. He said he could've fixed the brokerage if he would have had enough time.

"I knew I was not going to have enough time to fix it," he said. "So selling to BankAmerica was the only way to protect shareholders and employees."

A year before Thain's words would have sent me into a spitting fury. I wasn't protected. Nor was my family. Nor were more than half of all the adults in the U.S. labor force who, according to a Pew Research poll, experienced a work-related hardship—a period of unemployment, pay cut and involuntary move to part-time employment—since the recession had begun. On the personal front, more than seventy percent of Americans age forty and over said they had been affected by the economic crisis. More Americans still rent and still pay more than before as homeownership stays just beyond their reach.

And how do you accurately measure the intangible casualties of our great American fall? Poor health, troubled relationships, the shame of debt, of never having or being enough? Living in fear that you are just one crisis away from complete destruction?

Finding a sense of well-being, of wholeness, took time. The failures and heartache were buffered by the ever-present generosity of love. I held firmly to my unrelenting belief that weaknesses and strengths were all part of my story and it was high time I edited out a few leading characters. Like a well-groomed, custom-suited Wall Street banker.

I release you, John Thain, I said, as I pulled open the bedroom curtains and let the sun filter though the window, shining brightly.

Griffin received his sensors the next day. Gilly would finish her college semester the following week and return home for the summer. On her first full day back, she pulled two of our plastic lawn chairs from the back porch onto a sunny spot in the yard and invited me to join her. She brought up her paper and revealed she had been mad at me about that remark I'd made, but now neither one of us cared to remember. She told me she had revised the assignment and submitted a different version about me, the true one, she said. Would I like to read it?

"No, darling," I said, touching her hand. "It's your story, not mine."

So she was just being a normal nineteen-year-old daughter. Normal. How absolutely lovely.

And I would remember the night at the lake when I was so exhausted from being brave that I chose to be human, regaining my footing to pull myself out of the muck. I'd been packed up and moved out and reassembled enough to know what to keep and what to let go. Like the moving boxes in my life, I carefully placed the precious contents this side up so as not to damage what was inside. When everything was at stake– my marriage, my children's survival, my financial solvency, my emotional well-being—I adjusted and fought and scraped and healed, finding the best parts that defined me.

And, in the process, I discovered I could do the one thing that saved me every time.

I found a new way home.

Chapter 21

The Second Front Door: The Ballad of the Bucolic

Standing at the side entrance, Traci's hand shook as she turned the knob. The lock was sticking. It always had. One of the many quirky charms I loved about my former home by the hundred-year-old oak trees.

"I probably should have used the other front door," Traci said with a timid laugh as she jiggled the handle.

"Mike and I called this entrance the 'second front door' when telling visitors which one to use," I said, acknowledging the home's Cape Cod design with two front doors.

Following her into the family room, I noticed that my plaid sofa and love seat remained in the same location by the painted paneled wall with the pine green tufted ottoman centered between them. I meant, *her* sofa and love seat.

Traci gestured toward the kitchen, placing her purse on the side chair that backed up against the large window to the back porch. Hesitating, I wanted to peek into the porch that had launched a hundred dreams of its previous owner. But Traci was in a hurry. And I was feigning a nonchalant approach about the visit.

"I'm so sorry the house is a mess," she said, quickly walking through the kitchen into the hallway that led to my former library, now a guest room for her parents when they visited.

"Don't apologize. It looks lived in, the ultimate compliment," I said talking like an HGTV philosopher. I tried not to stare too long at any one spot for fear she'd notice I was as nervous as Traci seemed to be. She apologized for the slightly messy kitchen and the books left out on the daybed in the guest room and the antique piano in the adjoining living room, which she loved, but said it felt out of place in that room. The room where my family and I used to decorate our Christmas tree while listening to our customized iTunes holiday music of Bing Crosby's "White Christmas," Nat King Cole's "The Christmas Song," Larry

Carlton's version of "White Christmas" and our penultimate favorite, James Taylor's "Some Children See Him."

"It's really too big of a piece for this space," Traci said, rubbing her hand across the top of the stand-up piano.

"You should keep what you love. It tells a story," I said. Geeze, I sounded like a Buddhist Martha Stewart. Stop trying so hard, I thought to myself as I leaned around the corner to see the wood stairwell where Griffin and Gilly would slide down with their toboggan made out of blankets, gripping the cover for dear life, laughing their heads off as they bump-bump-bumped down the stairs.

"I'm thinking the rug could go in this room, but I'm not sure," Traci said directing me back to the study. Who would have thought, seven years since tearfully leaving this place, I would be standing inside it. Fate had brought me here. Well, a friend's estate sale down the street had brought Traci and I together as we peered through the tagged items for sale there, me finding a porcelain lamp for my rental's living room and Traci, a zebra-striped rug.

"Is zebra still in?" Traci had asked me, a fellow shopper once known in this neck of the woods for her design expertise.

"Hmmmm, I think so," I'd answered.

Traci then suggested we hop in her car and take a look inside her home. Just down the street. *Her* home. Not mine. We'd become friends since we'd met at the title office closing on what had been our home, signing the papers that meant I no longer owned it. No longer claimed it as mine.

I liked Traci. A lot. Damn it. She was gracious and funny and smart as hell. Even though ditching my antique side table to the side of the road could call into question one's character, I chose not to hold that against her. It belonged to her. That was part of the deal. She got the furniture she requested and the house and I got a different life, exiled far away from the house among the oaks.

What wasn't part of the deal was visiting her home. Although we met socially, over drinks, over dinner, over lunch, we never met at her house. Ever. She never said and I never offered how painful that would be for me. I suspected she knew. We lived in a community where secrets weren't secrets and loss was a communal kinship. And for that, I was grateful.

"Time has a way of healing things," Dad often said to me when I complained about a perceived hurt.

Standing in the house that Mike and I promised would be our forever home, I realized Dad was right. As usual. Traci must have sensed it, too, or she would not have invited me.

"Happy, Dad?" I whispered looking up to the ceiling while Traci pulled out her measuring tape to find the width of the study. Measurements I'd once taken when I considered adding carpet to the original oak floors before Mike jolted me into reality that oak floors should never be covered.

He was right.

I was wrong.

Then, he was wrong. And I was right. And we were both wrong. Both scarred. Wounded from losing something we always thought we'd have, a dream house with a porch decorated with white sheer curtains, a hand-painted table, wrought-iron chandeliers and a setting of some nineteenth-century china I'd never heard of, but would carry with me wherever I moved.

A house that once defined us.

As I walked through the rooms I once inhabited, I realized this house no longer owned *me*. My Christmas soundtrack had followed me wherever I went. From apartment number one to apartment number two to the House of Gray to the Tri-Level to Park View. To wherever was next. My family's traditions and memories, testimonies that we were a family of love and honor and gumption didn't disappear from view as we pulled out of Oak Lane Cottage for the last time.

Oak Lane Cottage. The plaque Mike hung to the brick wall's front entrance was still there, declaring itself a named presence among others. The house looked smaller than I remembered. And older. Like me.

"So here's where I'd put the rug," Traci said, standing in front of the daybed. "What do you think?"

I thought this is what it feels like to release a thousand burdens. From our very first move, I had morphed into a whole new being who knew the sum of my parts was only as good as the whole when I was around those who loved me. Regardless of where I lived.

"I think it would go perfectly here," I said, smiling. "Exactly where it belongs."

.   .   .   .   .   .

Returning to my rental that night, I collapsed on the couch in my home office. Mike and Gilly had gone to the YMCA to work out. Slipping off my shoes, I propped my bare feet onto the coffee table and accidentally nudged *The Style Book* onto the floor. "Time for you to go back where you belong," I said aloud as I placed the book on the top bookshelf. Above it was a plate, lit with the canned light above the shelves. I hadn't noticed it before, but must have hung it when we first moved in. It was the fourth Spode plate, a remnant from my Oak Lane Cottage porch makeover, a piece of china painted with a scene of a man and woman sitting on a lushly landscaped lawn with large ferns, willows and a stately pavilion. A scene of bucolic enchantment.

For an instant I was back at Orange Lake, standing with Dad, tossing our empty peanut shells in a bag as we looked at the tranquil waters nestled among weeping palm trees and perfumed orange blossoms.

"This is another place and time that inspired writers like Marjorie Kinnan Rawlings," Dad said, looking at the serene landscape in front of us just like the one the famous Highwayman artist had painted on canvas. "She wrote that she could never understand how someone could live without a piece of enchantment."

Looking up at my father, I remember never wanting to leave that sacred spot.

"Promise me you'll always keep a piece of enchantment wherever you go," Dad said, placing his hand on my heart.

"I promise, Dad," I said and threw an empty shell into the murky waters before we dusted off our jeans and left the lake as we had found it.

·   ·   ·   ·   ·   ·

Back in the rental of my home office, where the plastic floor curled up around the edges and the fluorescent ceiling light briefly flickered until it went dark, leaving only my desk lamp to illuminate the small room, I looked around. Pictures of Mike and Griffin and Gillian smiled at me from their framed positions on the bookshelf. Dad's self-published books about Old Ocala were stacked by family photos we had taken several months earlier when Griffin and Gilly were home from college. Dad lived hard times, sharing the truth as he knew it in his book about Ocala's Courthouse Square:

"Prosperity was just around the corner. What corner? The heart and soul of man would not be defeated. Walking the square on a Saturday afternoon were people who were not well off, but held onto an indestructible belief that things had to get better. The enigma of it all. That when life was hard and harsh, there was still tenderness and compassion. Through it all there was a time of innocence, fellowship, conviction and optimism. And we felt it on the Square."

·   ·   ·   ·   ·   ·

Doris Gates was an award-winning children's novelist who wrote a fictional account of the Great Depression years, *Blue Willow*. In her story, the blue willow plate is the prized possession of a young girl of a migrant worker's family. The cherished plate was given to the girl by her great-grandmother. The blue willow pattern of the plate represented the young girl's dream of a permanent home—a house beside a willow tree.

Standing by my desk, I turned on my iPod, choosing "Mangan Christmas Music" as Bing Crosby sang of days merry and bright. I turned down the air conditioner to cool off from the heat of the hot summer day. Christmas in July, I thought to myself. Why not?

Then I sat at my desk to write a note to a friend who was going through a difficult time. I picked up an ink pen from the three-plate server of Spode china, the one with lounging women and escaping pigs. The top plate was a scene of a well-dressed man standing alone and holding a tall rod. He had a look of contentment and pride, as if to say, "All I've got is this rod, but isn't it grand?"

Yes.

And it'll do.

Acknowledgments

I hope my gratitude for everyone who carried my family and me through the shadows and the light spills out on every page of this book.

To my husband, Mike Mangan, I owe you my heart not only for living through the hard parts of this story, but also for giving me the best parts, too. And you proved to be a keen manuscript editor. The very thought of you makes my heart sing, especially when you play our favorite John Coltrane song.

To my brave and beautiful children, Griffin and Gillian, for showing me and so many others what courage looks like. Griffin, I sang to you when you were born. Time after time, I tell myself that I am so lucky to love you. Gillian, I love you as deep as the ocean and as high as the sky from newborn to forever.

To my parents—my father, the original family writer, Sherman Yeary, Jr., my mentor and best spontaneous home renovation partner I ever had. I miss you. I love you. And my mother, Nel Yeary, who taught me to decorate with joy and a glue gun no matter where I live.

To my sisters Julie Moody and Cindy Fleetwood, who have moved me more than they cared to, but would gladly bring some duct tape and Diet Coke if I call upon their packing services again. You also are both extraordinary crisis managers for your baby sister.

To my niece, Holly Ignatz, thank you for being the supreme medical care networker with lightning speed response when my family needed it most. And my other sweet nieces, Valori Hall, Molly Moody and Lisa Lewis. Let's get together for another dance party.

To my nephew Joshua Yeary Moody, your spirit is with us. Our shared love of decorating with a vase of "sticks" stays with me always.

To my "other" children who began as friends of my children and have become part of my own: Allie Holland, Weston Truluck, Aakash Patel, Nick Wigelsworth, Bailey Underill, Madison Wolk, Marshall Wolk, Louie Kien, Alia French, Bailey LeFever, Lauren Anthony, Kaley Knapp, Julia Shea, Caitlyn Hall, and Will Glenn. Your Mama Mangz loves you.

I am indebted to my friends who show up and shower love, food, prayer, immensely thoughtful gestures and far too many "Welcome Home...Again" gifts, which I gladly accept. I love you, Pat and Gary Grunder, Sara and Chick Dassance, Vanessa and Blaine Baxley, Kelly and Jose Juarez, Laurie Ann and Dan Truluck,

Rusty Stanaland, Carolanne and Johnny Roberts, Cathy and Paul Clark, Barbara and Joe Kays, Ginger and Randy Cruze, Martha and Ron Barnwell, Debbie Bowe, Karey Holland, Stacy Strazis and Ruthy Young, Alex, Robin, Andrew, Will and Patrick Glenn, Carly, Luke and Bobby Pickels, Jenny Conley, PG Schafer, Valerie Strickland, Penny Villella, Karen Buss, Cynthia Edgar, Lisa and David Lancaster, Tracy Dreyfus, Julee McCammon, Mary and Charles Chazal, Violet and Rod Poetter, Cyndi and Bill Chambers, Eric Latimer, Laurie Zink, Laura Boisvert, Scott and Jo Wilkerson, Cameron Cooper, Melissa Seixas and Greg Feldman, and the WICS "Women in Charge" tribe— Jo Salyers, Kathy Judkins and Lori Boring.

Speaking of Sara and Chick, I must also include you with great affection for our Movie Club with Hellen and Walt Driggers. Movies and life aren't the same for Mike and me now that you have all moved away.

I wrote most of this book in a make-shift craft closet in my latest rental and with copious amounts of chocolate, but not without the creative sustenance from so many who cultivated my love of writing through the years. They include Steve Codraro for always making me look good in print and online and being the charter member of The Muses Group—with a shout-out to fellow member MaryAnn Desantis. Cynthia Barnett, your encouragement inspires me. Also, to Ann Hood's Pearl Street Writing Group members Charlotte DeKanter Chung and Sandy Silverman, as well as Connie May Fowler, Jamie Mark, Dean Blinkhorn, and John Dunn. To Jim Ross for my newspaper column. And a separate heaping of praise for and sentence with use of multiple exclamation marks for my friend and editor Dave Schlenker!!!!

While I'm praising wordsmiths, this book would not be possible without the keen editorial eye of the amazing Annie Tucker who now has to tolerate being my lifelong friend. I just hope we meet soon so we can laugh about ghosts and such. Is this a good time to tell you I've written a novel, too? And a special thanks to Susan Minnerly for her love and friendship.

Our family is grateful to the exceptional medical care for Griffin and Gillian by Dr. Himanshu Kairab, Dr. Paul Carney, Dr. Michael Haller, Dr. Jose Gaudier, Dr. Eduardo Cruz, Dr. Doug Murphy, Dr. George Jallo and so many compassionate health care professionals who are extraordinary not only because of what they do, but also because of who they are. They keep us inspired to believe we can find a cure for epilepsy and Type 1 diabetes.

Finally, I dedicate my story to anyone who feels like their world has been turned upside down with insurmountable challenges. Hold tight to faith, family and friends. May you find peace and happiness when pockets of light shine through.

View other Black Rose Writing titles at www.blackrosewriting.com/books and
use promo code **PRINT** to receive a **20% discount** when purchasing.

BLACK ROSE
writing™

CPSIA information can be obtained
at www.ICGtesting.com
Printed in the USA
FFHW01n1431160718
47407436-50592FF